COMICS ART

Paul Gravett

COMICS ART

Tate Publishing

ACKNOWLEDGEMENTS

First published 2013 by order of the Tate Trustees
by Tate Publishing, a division of Tate Enterprises Ltd,
Millbank, London SW1P 4RG
www.tate.org.uk/publishing

A catalogue record for this book is
available from the British Library
ISBN 978-1-84976-056-0

Designed by Peter Stanbury
Colour reproduction by DL Imaging, London
Printed in Hong Kong by Printing Express

Many people have kindled and rekindled my passion for comics over my lifetime and this book owes a huge amount to them. Whenever my interest threatened to wane, someone would introduce me to yet another facet of this inexhaustible medium.

My mother took me to my first comics shop, Dark They Were And Golden-Eyed in London's seedy Soho, and to my first comics art exhibition, Aargh! at the Institute of Contemporary Arts. Mal Burns was my initial guide into the self-published small press scene. Maurice Horn unveiled a whole planet of comics in his seminal World Encyclopedia. Joe Ekers ushered me into the vibrant history of American newspaper strips. Richard Edington showed me my first 500-page manga weekly and joined me on my first serious expedition to Paris to buy bande dessinée albums. Serge and Henriette Boissevain gave me my first job in comics publishing. Ian Rakoff deepened my understanding of the classics. Tim Webber built and ran my website www.paulgravett.com, and Russell Willis of Panel Nine helped me take the plunge into today's digital comics. It is thanks to these and many others that instead of growing out of comics, I have been able to grow up with them.

I am also enormously grateful to Chelsey Fox, and to Roger Thorp, Nicola Bion, Sarah Tucker, Juliette Dupire and the team at Tate Publishing, to all of the writers, artists, publishers, dealers, collectors, researchers and scholars without whom this book would not exist, and in particular to my partner Peter Stanbury for his design, ingenuity and patience.

Finally, I am dedicating this book to the memories of Les Coleman and Kim Thompson, two friends and inspiring connoisseurs who never lost their passion.

Paul Gravett

FRONT COVER
The Comix Factory
Joost Swarte, colouring by Françoise Mouly
Detail from the cover of *RAW*, vol.1, no.2, 1980

BACK COVER
The Rut
Dave McKean
From *Hypercomics* at The Pump House Gallery,
London, 2010

FRONTISPIECE
Untitled
Charles Burns
Originally published in *Artforum*, 1991

CONTENTS

ENCOMPASSING COMICS:
THE OTHER HISTORY

Krazy Kat
George Herriman, 22 August 1936
Original artwork

Listen closely. It never stops. You can almost make out the scratching of pens and pencils onto paper, the tapping of typewriters, the clicking of computers, the buzz of printing presses and binders, all the assorted sound effects of writers, artists and printers creating more comics every minute all over the world. The sheer profusion of comics, past and present, can make it a challenge to orientate oneself in this dizzying, ever-expanding territory. It's easy to get confused or lost. And then, a shaft of light sweeps around, circling and slicing through the darkness, lighting up the landscape. The beam comes from a lighthouse, there not only to help guide those at sea to safety. This particular lighthouse guides in another way, as a library, a beacon of knowledge, sending out its illumination far and wide. Within its circular walls and cornerless rooms, like some Borghesian fantasy, shelf after shelf is crammed with hundreds of remarkable comics, previously unknown, never published anywhere, except in this fictional New Zealand coastal hamlet. Welcome to Hicksville, a sort of secret comics paradise. Listen in to its librarian-cum-lighthouse keeper's guided tour of the bookcases, given to an incredulous journalist visiting from America:

> The official history of comics is a history of frustration. Of unrealised potential. Of artists who never got the chance to do that magnum opus. Of stories that never got told – or else were bowdlerised by small-minded editors ... A medium locked into a ghetto and ignored by countless people who could have made it sing ... Well, here it is. The other

history of comics. The way it should have been. The masterpieces. The great novels. The pure expressions. Going back hundreds of years.[1]

When envisaging the location of his comics utopia for the 1998 graphic novel *Hicksville* (p.8), New Zealander Dylan Horrocks did not concoct some spectacular wonderland, but chose a more modest ideal sanctuary for his beloved medium, closer to home, in humble, humdrum Hicksville. Rather than elevating comics into some palatial museum of fine art, he chose a library, a haven for books and bibliophiles. Hicksville's inhabitants, all devotees and connoisseurs, set aside divisive differences in taste to unite in their shared passion and their protectiveness of the town's priceless locally printed treasures. Among others, the librarian refers the stunned reporter to fifteen or sixteen comics by Pablo Picasso:

> Here's a 48-page comic he did with Lorca. Etchings, mostly. I reckon it's one of his best ... He did his first as a present for [George] Herriman. Then there were a couple written [for him] by Gertrude Stein, and the rest are mostly pornographic books.

Horrocks makes these imaginary works sound almost plausible. In fact, in a parallel world, in the 'other history of comics', they could so easily have been created. In *The Autobiography of Alice B. Toklas*, Gertrude Stein recorded Picasso's enthusiasm in 1906 for the bold, brash cartooning which he saw in the 'Sunday Funnies', big broadsheet supplements of 'polychromatic effulgence' from

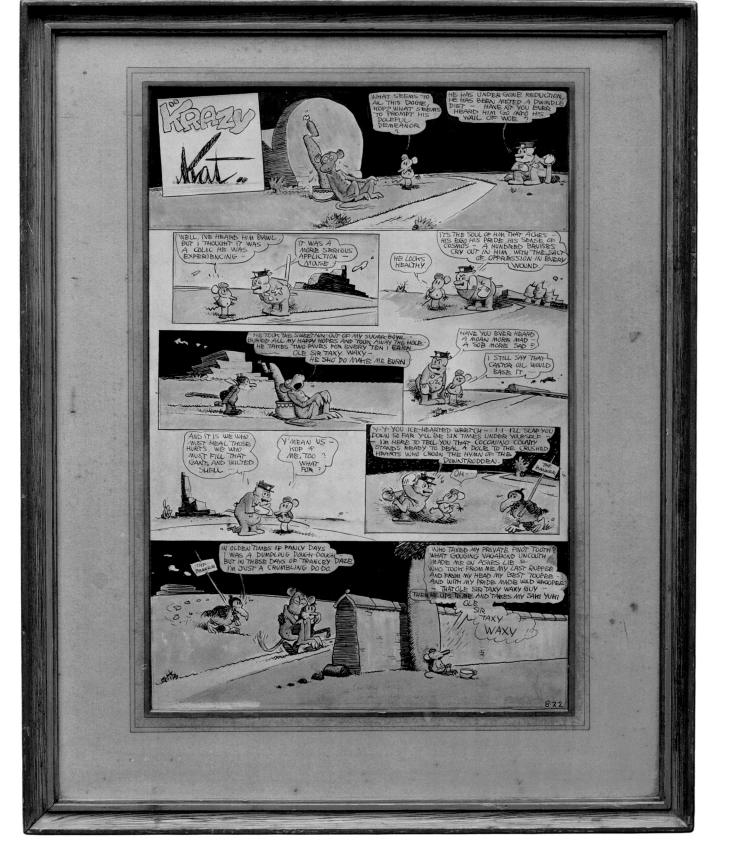

early twentieth-century American newspapers shipped to Stein in Paris. In *The Salon* (right), Nick Bertozzi speculates how Picasso might have found a solution to his portrait of Stein from the dots for eyes used in comics. Although Picasso said 'The only thing I regret in my life is not having made comics'[2] he came close at least twice. He wrote and drew a six-panel travelogue of a 1904 trip between Barcelona and Paris, and in 1937 a heartfelt poem to accompany a pair of fundraising,

pro-Republican prints, *Dream and Lie of Franco*. Their nine-panel grids savaged the Spanish leader and lamented the destruction of Guernica, anticipating Picasso's masterpiece condemning the brutal bombing of the town.

It is tantalising to imagine what other wonders wait to be read in Hicksville's impossible library, but there is also a wistful, even sad realisation that its archive symbolises what might have been, but never was. There is tinge of anger in the librarian's commentary too, a rallying cry for change and liberation in the medium. Fortunately, as this book will show, change has come or seems imminent, but struggles and setbacks remain, however, to this day.

One of the wellsprings of comics is the political and social cartoon and caricature, notorious for their role as mocking court jester. Fears about the subversive effects of comics on their public accompanied them from their earliest days, and still persist. Throughout their history, comics have been co-opted to serve a country's dominant ideology, most obviously as wartime propaganda, official educational messages or as weapons in cultural imperialism, but they can also question and threaten authority.

Comics are also closely associated with childhood, and with the related world of children's picture books. They are perhaps the first stories and artwork we are able to choose for ourselves. Some of the greatest comics, past and present, are designed for kids and yet can be savoured by all ages. But it

was partly out of this association that the false assumption arose that the medium of comics was designed solely for the young, and the subliterate. This has made comics an easy target and scapegoat for self-professed moral guardians and opportunistic politicians and lobbyists, who condemn them when they dare to challenge the status quo and address more mature subjects. Notably, after the Second World War, establishment forces in numerous nations, sometimes forging unlikely alliances, for example between the Church and the Communist Party, and often strengthened by local protectionist pressures, constrained the content of comics to sometimes ludicrous infantilism, through legislation, self-regulatory codes by publishers, market pressures and self-censorship. Strictures vary, of course, but it is hard to think of another medium that has been consigned for so long to the juvenile or had to

prove so often that it can and should be allowed to tackle adult themes.

Similarly, despite the term being derived from the comical, the medium of comics is not confined to humour. Nor is it restricted to a genre, such as the superhero stories. It is a medium open to covering almost every subject using visual and often verbal language. The comics artform is not sub-literature, kitsch or Pop art, nor simply a collection of storyboards for a film on paper, but an autonomous art with particular systems and cultures. The global cross-pollination of influences has a long history, although the speed and spread of its transformation and transnationalisation have greatly increased in recent years. For example, few could have anticipated that Japanese comics would become so successful in translation, even in their original, right-to-left, 'authentic' reading order, capturing forty per cent of the French comics market. Similarly, while print is far from dead, many consumers are turning from paper to pixels or growing up exclusively reading on screens, phones, tablets and other platforms from an exponential explosion of webcomics and other new digital variations. Since the 1960s, the growth in comics conventions and festivals big and small around the world, from Algeria to the Arctic, has helped to bring together professionals, fans, academics, media and the general public in stimulating exchanges of projects, properties, trends and techniques. By further connecting readers, creators and researchers, the internet has facilitated a boom in studies into comics from a wide variety of cultures and specialities. Out of this came the first international conference in London in 2010 on comics and medicine. Katie Green conveys her struggles with anorexia with arresting symbolism and candour in *Lighter Than My Shadow* (right), one of a burgeoning sector of autobiographical graphic novels which can instil more empathy in medical professionals for those fighting illness or caring for others. The first seminars on comics and sculpture in Leeds in 2011, and comics and the law in London in 2013, are cross-disciplinary encounters almost unthinkable a decade before.

Setting aside the apparent universality of comics without words, the written languages within comics remain a hurdle, if not a barrier, to understanding a field as vast as this. It is little wonder most readers stick to what they know or can easily read. As a result, no matter how international and interdisciplinary the dedicated websites, forums, journals, conferences and courses strive to be, many who create and study comics have only a partial grounding upon which to build, hampering broader informed debate. Often the body of knowledge necessary to underpin enquiry is only partially known or reduced to a narrow, repeated set of 'facts'. Yet the historical, factual approach is not the only way to investigate the medium. From the plethora of recent textbooks and papers on the subject, Gregory Steirer has distinguished five additional approaches to comics scholarship – sociocultural, ideological, auteurist, formalist, and industrial – each distinct and arising, usually, from particular academic

disciplines: 'Sociocultural comics scholarship, it turns out, is usually produced by historians, ideological by sociologists, auteurist and formalist by literature or cinema scholars, and industrial by media scholars'.[3] While all these diverse perspectives and expertise can cumulatively deepen our understanding and appreciation of comics, a coherent overview and consensus remains elusive. At least the debate is underway. This book will be trying on all six of Steirer's different disciplinary hats to examine some of the cutting-edge innovations in the practices and theories of twenty-first-century comics, considering where the medium has got to now and where it is heading next. Perhaps from here we can begin to glimpse that bigger picture of what makes comics an art.

There are obvious tensions and contradictions across the spectrum of comics, which spans from the most industrial mass entertainment to the most personal artistic expression. Innovation and bestsellers can occur anywhere, although the boldest experimentation has generally been more possible outside the limitations of the largely conformist, commercial market. The medium's adult potential was explored most spectacularly in America's underground comix movement of the 1960s and 1970s, distributed through drug paraphernalia stores and the counterculture network. The movement soon gave rise to parallel responses worldwide, and from members of the avant-garde of contemporary art, literature and poetry, such as Guy Peellaert, William

Lighter Than My Shadow
Katie Green, 2013

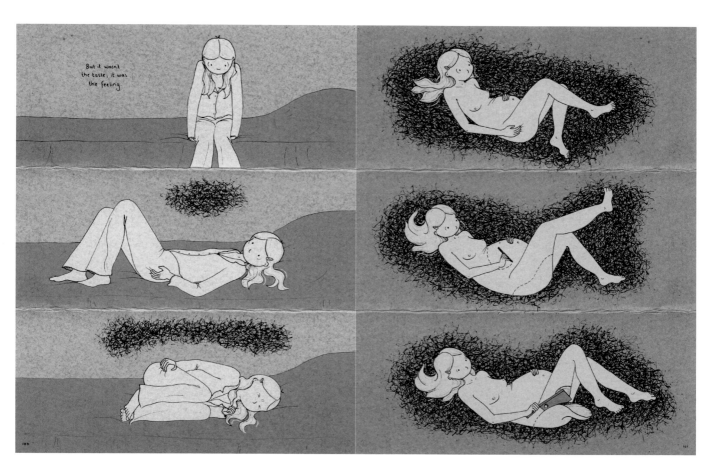

Burroughs, Dino Buzzati, Philip Guston, Julio Cortazár, Pushwagner and Martin Vaughn-James. His 1975 'visual novel' *The Cage* (pp.114–15)shows nothing living, only interiors and exteriors, like art installations. Other writers and artists have attempted to subvert from within the mainstream and push against formulas to bring new vigour to apparently moribund genres.

To understand how this greater creative freedom has become more widespread in comics, it is useful to get some perspective on the shifts in the production, publishing, printing, marketing and reception of comics and how these have impacted on the writers and artists who create them. Comics is not unusual among the arts in being both an art and a business. In their authorship, comics can be the product of a single, irreplaceable individual handling every step, like Charles M. Schulz on 'Peanuts', or one close-knit, almost symbiotic writer-artist partnership, like the Argentine duo Carlos Sampayo and José Muñoz on 'Alack Sinner'. Comics can also be the collaborative output of a studio of assistants realising a master artist's plans, such as Frank Hampson on 'Dan Dare' or Hergé on *Tintin*, or a segmented assembly line of editors, writers, pencillers, inkers, letterers, colourists and designers, often the norm in high-volume American comic books or Japanese manga. Whatever the process, it is no guarantee of popularity or quality.

Hergé is an unmistakable inspiration for the Dutch cartoonist and designer

Joost Swarte, whose detailed interior view forms the cover to this book. Swarte applies the satirical over-complication with which W. Heath Robinson and Rube Goldberg ridiculed the early twentieth-century machine age to fantasise about how America's daily newspaper comic strips of that era might have been manufactured in a 'Comix Factory' as spacious as a movie lot. Instead of a lone cartoonist toiling at a drawing board, Swarte suggests an elaborate procedure requiring an army of look-alike actors (and animals), technicians, props – and one caffeine-stoked scriptwriter struggling to come up with another episode. This is fanciful farce, of course, but it reflects the increasing industrialisation of comics led by America, once the same strips could be sold to more and more papers and spun off into other lucrative media and merchandise.

Before this, during the late nineteenth and early twentieth centuries, there was a surprising amount of freedom for solo cartoonists to experiment in America's Sunday newspapers, many printed in dazzling or subtly graduated colours that, the press advertising claimed, would '... make the rainbow look like a lead pipe!' Pages had to be filled and the opportunities attracted cartoonists, illustrators and artists of varying backgrounds and skills. Though they built on precedents from European narrative prints and cartoon magazines, the form and the format offered creators regular, spacious virgin territory ripe for exploration. Some might dabble in a quirky feature, only to drop it, perhaps after a brief run, never to attempt it again, like Charles Forbell's strikingly composed 'Naughty Pete' which lasted eighteen weeks, or Herbert Crowley's eccentric bestiary 'The Wiggle Much', a mere thirteen weeks.

Other newspaper cartoonists like George Herriman were able to work on comics their whole lives. In an uncommon act of patronage, press magnate William Randolph Hearst so adored Herriman's inimitable 'Krazy Kat' (p.7) that he insisted the strip appear and underwrote it until the cartoonist's death in 1944. Secure with a lifetime contract and creative freedom, Herriman could take his Coconino County cast wherever he wanted. He believed: 'People don't know what they want. And if they get an entirely new taste of something that's good, they'll want it until they find something better. But we've got to give them the initial taste before they start clamoring for more.' Sadly, 'Krazy Kat' was too new and too much of an acquired taste. The strip never won the public's heart like its contemporaries 'Felix the Cat' or 'Mickey Mouse', but it was admired by the cognoscenti. When Herriman gave one of his large full-page Sunday artworks to friends, he would sometimes hand-colour the piece with home-made paints partly based on local Native American pigments and decorate the frame, a rare instance of a comics artist at the time consciously turning his commercial art made for reproduction into a unique, hand-made work of art. The example on page 7, dedicated with 'Affectionate greetings, friend' in Navajo to the American typography commentator Beatrice

Warde, was miraculously rescued from a London house clearance around 1986.

The art and business of comics were forever changed by syndication. Hearst's King Features, founded in 1915, began servicing not only papers in cities across America but around the world. Real money started pouring in for both publishers and cartoonists. The increased demand for a constant supply of strips in Sunday and daily newspapers, and fresh material for their offshoots and rivals, comic books, meant that publishers could not always rely on a single creator. Some cartoonists would employ assistants to take on parts of the workload, filling in areas of black, inking pencil drawings, drawing backgrounds, handling lettering. The solitary artistic genius in charge of every aspect was giving way to a more pragmatic, step-by-step assembly line. The sweatshop system was not so different from the tailoring and garment industry – ironically, the very trade which two tailors' sons, Jack Kirby and Joe Simon, a successful young comic book team, were so keen to avoid.

One result of accelerated production was the invention of the previously unknown job of comics scriptwriter. In 1934, King Features secured the bestselling crime writer Dashiell Hammett to devise a new daily serial, 'Secret Agent X-9', though he seems to have struggled with the medium and left for the more profitable film industry. The gradual increased reliance on writers paved the way for illustrators happy to realise other people's tales, often

... at its core, the cylinder too is poised between rotations ...

transfixed upon its waste, within the monotony of its wall ...

... only one object still commands attention ...

... rooted firmly in the centre of the plain ...

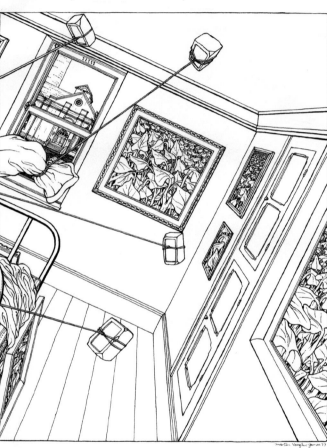

adept in polished draughtsmanship, but lacking confidence in stories of their own. Creators of comics no longer had to be jacks of all trades, but could master just one – a penciller, an inker completing those pencils for reproduction, a colourist, a letterer. Successful cartoonists could divide their labour among uncredited 'ghost artists'. Don Sherwood reportedly managed to keep all his assistants separate and unknown to each other so they would co-produce his 'Dan Flagg' strip (1963–7) for him, while he claimed the sole byline, full credit and most of the money for himself.

It was still possible to craft a comic entirely alone, but the expanding industry tended to prioritise printing and distribution deadlines over anything else. Words, as in scripts, became the starting point of many comics, with in-house editors tweaking the texts before supplying them to artists. Entertaining Comics (EC) would insert all the words, often quite florid, into captions and dialogue balloons, leaving the remainder of the panel blank for the illustrator to fill in. This makes some economic sense – why pay artists to draw what will end up being obscured by lettering? Great writers would emerge who understood the visual power of comics, but it was not uncommon in writer-led comics for artists to be unable to adjust the pacing and panels, owing to limited, pre-set page counts and panel layouts for stories. The words did so much of the work that the pictures served more as decorative props and prompts. When presented with Al Feldstein's script for

'Master Race', the tale of a German concentration camp officer being recognised by a Holocaust survivor on the New York subway, Bernard Krigstein had to beg to be given two extra pages, eight rather than six, to expand it and let it 'sing' (right). In this rare case, he was allowed to fragment the Nazi's climactic death from an accidental fall under a subway train into wordless, moment-by-moment slivers, echoed in the refracted passengers in the eleventh panel. The impact is jarringly powerful. For comics to become a more flexible and expressive medium, the pictures also had to be permitted to tell the story.

To cope with deadline-driven pressures, the Marvel method, already in practice before the 1960s, came to avoid detailed scripts and therefore empowered the artists to some extent by letting them pace and illustrate the comic from an outline or plot idea. As a result, Jack Kirby, Steve Ditko and others were given increasing rein to produce more than accompanying illustrations and could channel their innate narrative skills. But at Marvel, artists had no final say. That went to chief writer and self-appointed editor, answerable to nobody else, Stan Lee. A rare surviving photocopy of Kirby's 'pencils' shows that by 1968 he was not working from a full script but only the thinnest of plotlines, and yet was transforming this into complete narrative images with his dialogue and directions in the margins (p.19). The main creative tasks of writing were done, which Lee has only to follow, more or less. Lee would leave barely any space uncovered by speech and thought bubbles. In an early *X-Men*,

would write more visually for American comic books, from Archie Goodwin, Alan Moore and Grant Morrison to Brian Michael Bendis, Ed Brubaker, Bill Willingham and Brian Moore, all of whom have written and illustrated their own comics. Knowing how to draw, they can write for an artist, trusting them to tell the story visually as required. Equally vital has been artists gaining the confidence to write their own material. A prime example is the late French master of *bande dessinée*, Jean Giraud, illustrator only on the 'Lieutenant Blueberry' western series written by Jean-Michel Charlier. Giraud adopted his Moebius pen-name originally to author some humorous solo short pieces. He later used this secret identity, his other side of the strip, to work on four silent, fully painted short reveries in *Arzach*, unlike anything seen in comics before, and on his improvised *Airtight Garage*. He would grow into a visionary universe-builder. Other self-aware, self-analysing practitioners have become theorists, scrutinising the deceptively 'simple' medium of comics. This process began with a founding father of the form, Rodolphe Töpffer, who published his *Essai de Physiognomonie* in Geneva in 1845, and has been continued by Will Eisner, starting in his *Comics and Sequential Art* (1985), and currently by Scott McCloud, Benoît Peeters, Jean-Christophe Menu and Chris Ware, among others.

Returning to the Hicksville lighthouse library, no doubt it also contains comics by Picasso's fellow countryman, Salvador Dalí. When he was twelve, Dalí had drawn comics for his sister, and he

his verbosity so inflated a balloon that the villain Magneto is all but obscured by his own hyperbole. When Kirby choreographed a nine-panel page of a balletic combat between Captain America and Batroc, so dynamic it had no need for words, Lee could not resist adding a jaunty footnote extolling Kirby's genius. Compared to typically lengthier Japanese comics which freely used wordless panels and sequences since the 1950s, for years the rule in the majority of American comic books and Western output was 'in the beginning was the word', and not the picture.

Fortunately, this would change as more writers with their own artistic gifts

'Master Race' from Impact 1
Alfred Feldstein (writer)
and Bernard Krigstein (artist), April 1955

ABOVE:
Installations at the 'Bande dessinée et figuration narrative' exhibition
Louvre, Paris, 1967

RIGHT:
'When Wakes the Sleeper!' from Captain America 101
Jack Kirby (writer and artist) and Stan Lee (writer), May 1968
Original artwork

designed comic-like storyboards, notably in 1945–6 for 'Destino', an animated short film project for Walt Disney, eventually released in 2003. While visiting Paris in 1967, Dalí envisaged a utopia for comics, not built on wonders from the past, but realised in the far future and spearheaded, of course, by Dalí himself. That year, the Louvre staged its first exhibition about comics, *Bande dessinée et figuration narrative* (above) in which designer Isabelle Chavarot mounted monochrome blow-ups of panels onto boards and coloured tulle and collated different uses of texts and balloons onto the faces of sculptures in the 'Hall of Cubes'. Dalí visited Librairie Antica, one of the earliest Parisian bookshops for collectable comics. Clutching a sampling of these rarities, while balancing a carafe of iced water on his head to

cool his boiling brain, Dalí proclaimed to his companion, Amanda Lear:

> Comics will be the culture of the year 3794. So you have 1,827 years in advance, which is good. In fact, it leaves me the time I need to create a collage with these eighty comics I am taking with me. This will be the birth of Comics Art, and on this occasion we will hold a grand opening with my divine presence on March 4th 3794 at 19.00 hours precisely.[4]

Dalí's enthusiasm for 'Comics Art' proved fleeting. In 1973, French-Canadian editor Michel Choquette visited Dalí in an attempt to persuade him to join in *The Someday Funnies*, a seemingly impossible comics anthology about the 1960s. Choquette recalls: 'I spent an afternoon with Salvador Dalí and his

As one tipping point after another is proving, comics are already the culture of today. Robert Storr, curator of the Art Spiegelman show *Making Maus*, the first exhibition of comics at New York's Museum of Modern Art in 1991, is convinced: 'Someday soon the citadels of culture will be forced to open their gates and let "the barbarians" in – only to discover how sophisticated they are.'[5] That day is today. In 2011, Robert Crumb and Art Spiegelman had major retrospectives at the Palais de Tokyo and Pompidou Centre in Paris, while in 2013, Daniel Clowes' one-man show came to the Museum of Contemporary Art in his birthplace, Chicago. Since 2007, the Louvre itself has commissioned a graphic novelist each year to interpret its collections and in 2012–13 devoted a gallery to Enki Bilal's portraits of fictional ghosts related to twenty-two works of art.

Opportunities for comics are greater than ever. As *Hicksville*'s author Dylan Horrocks sums up, he embraces the creative freedom they offer him: 'There are times when I'll want to let words take over completely, and other times when I speak entirely with pictures. I see my job as putting things on paper ... I feel no need to limit what shape those things can take.'[6] Another history of comics is being written before our eyes. As the shelves of our libraries, bookshops and homes pile up with further 'pure expressions', books that are not imaginary or missed opportunities but entirely, excitingly real, any of us can live in a Hicksville of our own choosing. Listen closely again and you will also hear a medium in full song.

wife, Gala, drinking pink champagne by his penis-shaped pool, as he explained why he was too important to draw a strip for me but would gladly do a poster for the book if my publishers were rich enough.' Nearly forty years later, in 2011, Choquette had his dream project finally published, an idiosyncratic time capsule but also a prophetic coming-together between comics creators and such luminaries of the times as Federico Fellini, Tom Wolfe and Frank Zappa.

It seems probable that Dalí had been inspired by Winsor McCay's nightmarish strips 'Dream of The Rarebit Fiend' (right) when devising his surrealist movie with Luis Buñuel, *L'Age d'Or* (1936). Among others, scenes in the 1906 episode opposite of a man kicking a dog, punching a blind man, striking an old woman and bundling her out of the window recur in the seminal film. As for Dalí's prediction, he was accurate in all but the year. We don't have to wait centuries for his triumphant ectoplasmic return.

ABOVE:
Art Spiegelman at CO-MIX:
A Retrospective of Comics, Graphics and Scraps
Musée de la bande dessinée, Angoulême,
January 2012

RIGHT:
Dream of the Rarebit Fiend
Winsor McCay ('Silas'), 4 August 1906
Original artwork

2

'Seicherls schreklichstes Badeabenteuer'
(Seicherl's Most Terrifying Aquatic Adventure)
in DAS KLEINE BLATT
Ladislaus Kmoch, 1934–5

A single piece of paper tried to rewrite the history of comics, when it was signed on 30 October 1989 at the Lucca Comics Festival in Italy. A quorum of experts was convened at an official summit to determine once and for all exactly when comics had been born. To do this, they had to define the medium's essential properties and decide where they first came together. After days of deliberation, they emerged with an agreement. It read: 'The eleven international specialists, gathered in Lucca, establish by absolute majority that 1896 was the year of birth of the comics. This was the year in which, through the character of the Yellow Kid, the comics, assuming the expressive contributions provided previously by creators from various countries, launched those special linguistic characteristics which would transform it into a new medium of communication.'

In their judgement, the crucial turning point was a much-vaunted episode – recovered from fading, crumbling newsprint – of 'The Yellow Kid', the American newspaper character by Richard Fenton Outcault published on Sunday 25 October 1896 in the *New York Journal* (see p.25). Those 'special lingustic characteristics' to which they referred included the first use of speech balloons by this character since he debuted discreetly in the *New York World* on 5 May 1895. From this beginning, the Yellow Kid had only ever communicated his reactions in broad Irish brogue roughly scrawled by hand onto his long yellow nightshirt, like a street hawker wearing a sandwich board. He would often break the 'fourth wall' and beam out at the readers, his shirt's bright, bold colouring catching their eye. As his remarks would be rewritten from one appearance to the next, his whole outfit operates as one peculiar balloon as if he is wearing, even embodying, his own words. The bald, flap-eared urchin proved so popular, he was used on big billboard posters for the *New York Journal*'s 'Colored Comic Supplement' (p.24).

At first, the Yellow Kid had appeared only in single-panel captioned cartoons, expanding later to large scenes in colour teeming with the textual signage, advertising hoardings and raucous details of street life. Crucially, in a break from these single images, Outcault came up with the first in a series of half-page, five-picture sequences, additional to his main cartoons, proof of his child-star's growing appeal. It is striking that the cheeky tyke appears in the initial 1896 example entirely alone save for one prop, his new phonograph (p.25). He appears five times on a blank page without any of the usual urban background or chaotic crowds, to demonstrate the novel machine. Because Outcault has to portray sound, he initially shows the balloons floating out of the phonograph's horn extolling the newspaper's colour supplement and the Yellow Kid himself. Then, in the punchline scene, a balloon sprouts from a parrot, the hidden speaker, who waddles out of the phonograph box, and another sprouts from a surprised Yellow Kid, whose shirt is suddenly blank as he finally speaks for himself, complaining: 'De phonograph is a great invention – NIT! I don't think.'

Seicherls schrecklichstes Badeabenteuer.

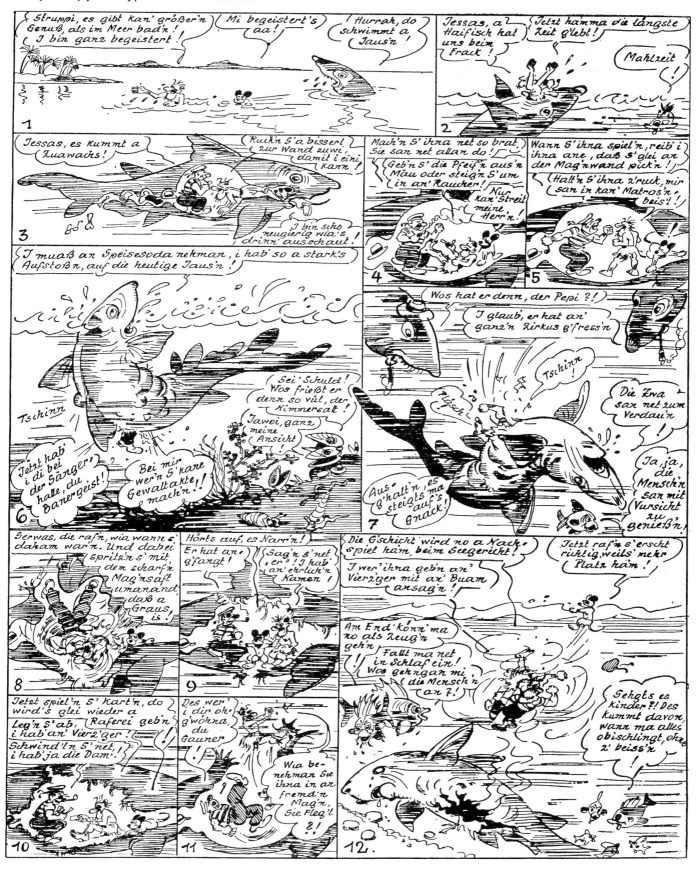

New York City billboards
Uncredited, c.1896

There was a 'great invention' in this short strip, the sequential use of speech balloons to bring characters alive, although Outcault was slow to experiment with it further. He would come up with only nine more extra comics sequences of this type for Sundays, several featuring that chatty parrot, but the Kid lost his new-found voice, piping up only once more to escape the blame by claiming, 'It's all de goat's fault'. As for the rest of Outcault's seven other sporadic sequential episodes, some in no more than two panels, the Kid lets his shirt do all the talking again. Still, the potential of real-time sequential speech-balloon dialogue in comics had been demonstrated.

The experts' choice of 1896 was not accidental, because it conveniently allowed the centenary of comics to be celebrated in 1996, seven years after 1989 and in enough time to prepare commemorative stamps, exhibitions

and conferences in the USA and elsewhere. It also confirmed America as the birthplace of modern comics, affirming the contention that they were a uniquely American art form. It is no coincidence that of the eleven signatories, three came from the USA, and notably absent was anyone from Asia. There was one dissenter, the British comics historian Denis Gifford, who provocatively signed the agreement 'Ally Sloper 1876', to credit the popular British character who had existed twenty years before the Yellow Kid. Gifford could have written an even earlier year, 1867, when the character first appeared in *Judy* magazine. No doubt Gifford had tried arguing the case for Sloper as the progenitor of the form, certainly as a key recurring character (another widely held criterion). The debate would have been that Marie Duval's humorous multi-panelled strips about this loveable rogue from the East End of London made no use of speech balloons, only typeset narration beneath the panels.

Looking back, speech balloons seem to have been with us long before 1896 as, for example, explanatory comments or so-called 'loops' in nineteenth-century American political cartoons, or wafting aloft in clusters within eighteenth-century British satirical prints, or earlier still as lettered parchment scrolls or phylacters, or ribbon- or banner-like 'banderoles' employed in medieval art and illumination. Although these can be utilised across a suite of images, on closer reading it becomes clear that they rarely represented a true expressive conversation unfolding over real time, but functioned rather as a labelling device. Belgian researcher Thierry Smolderen identifies the label as a precursor of the speech balloon, but wholly distinct from it. '[The label] evoked the self-presentational written banners of the frozen *tableau vivant*. It was in its nature to be embedded

in static coded pictures cut [off] from the physical world – pictures without past or future, whose original function, in the Baroque age, was to represent abstract and timeless truths. Pictorial stories were the last places where a reader would have expected to find a label. The modern speech balloon, however, evokes the opposite image, of a dynamic world, pregnant with narrative developments; the balloon is perfectly synchronised with the sequential template of pantomime action.'[1]

So those experts in Lucca were on the right track; something extraordinary had happened in that modest yet seminal 'Yellow Kid' example, as an act of speech became a symbol of speech. Perhaps it needed the invention of the phonograph to record and transmit sound in order to stimulate the evolution of the speech balloon to represent sound physically,

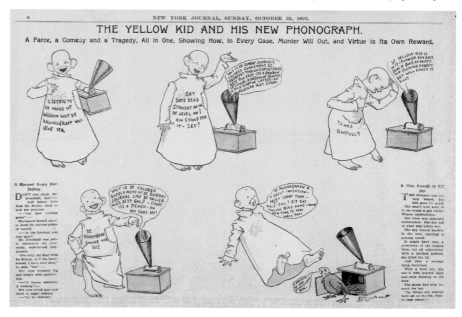

The Yellow Kid and His New Phonograph
Richard Fenton Outcault, 25 October 1896

graphically and temporally. It was an innovation which other American newspapermen would build on soon after, notably Frederick Burr Opper in 'Happy Hooligan' (1900) and the parodic patter of overblown French politesse in 'Alphone and Gaston' (1901), as well as Outcault's 'Buster Brown' (1902). The speech balloon, and its relative the thought balloon, often in the shape of a cloud, produce a transformative effect when integrated inside the panel. They seem to give a voice and consciousness to the simplest of cartoon figures. By emitting from their mouths and brains, dialogues and musings reinforce the effect of time passing inside a panel and between panels. In theory, reading texts and reading drawings within panels can combine as an experience much more smoothly than when having to navigate between separated and isolated pictures and words. As such, for many these balloons have become emblematic, if not defining, of comics. It is perfectly possible to create comics without them, of course, whether entirely textless and solely visual, or by placing narration only in captions.

There was considerable resistance to integrating balloons into modern comics. In Italy, comics would come to be known as 'fumetti' or 'little clouds of smoke', specifically after balloons, but initially their ubiquity caused concerns among educationalists and parents. When early twentieth-century American newspaper strips such as 'The Katzenjammer Kids', 'Felix the Cat' or later 'Mickey Mouse', arrived for example in Italy and Germany, their speech balloons were removed

from the panels and replaced by commentary below, sometimes in rhyme. Such was the influence of Germany's pioneer Wilhelm Busch, famed for his 1865 success *Max and Moritz (A Story of Seven Boyish Pranks)*, that his balloonless approach became the norm and would largely stall the medium and obstruct the acceptance by creators, publishers and readers of speech balloons in the German language until 1930, when the Austrian Ladislaus Kmoch helped to popularise them through his 'Tobias Seicherl' strips (p.23). In Britain as late as the 1950s, several children's weekly comics persisted in running largely redundant blocks of type under the panels, when the story could be clearly understood from the images and balloons above.

In parallel, vibrant and thoroughly modern comics sprang up which embraced the fresh audio-visual immediacy of the medium. Founding fathers of the form such as Milton Caniff in America (right), Hergé in Belgium and Osamu Tezuka in Japan took prime inspiration from theatre and the movies and sought to reproduce their illusion of reality. In fact, comics were already 'talkies' years before sound became standard in film, and they had helped prepare the public for the arrival of talking cinema. So it's no surprise that the influences between cinema and comics flowed in both directions. When the young Orson Welles released his first feature film, *Citizen Kane*, in 1941, its progressive camera angles and effects created a sensation among apprentice American cartoonists struggling to draw comic books often with little or

Terry and the Pirates
Milton Caniff, 24 September 1939
Original artwork

39

no training. Some of these tyros went back again and again to learn from Welles's masterpiece. Films were great teachers, helping novices select each 'shot' and encouraging them to think visually and sequentially. For many, composing their pages was like making movies on paper. Jack Kirby, for one, recalled, 'I was a movie person. I think it was one of the reasons I drew comics.' Hergé heralded his scouting hero Totor in 1926, three years before Tintin, with the billing, 'United Rovers present an extrasuperfilm' by 'Hergé, director'.

Equally, Welles is known to have enjoyed American newspaper strips. Among Milton Caniff's papers at the Ohio State University Billy Ireland Cartoon Library and Museum is a letter sent to him on Mercury Theatre stationery from Welles. It is a thank you note for Caniff's gift of an original drawing of his sultry oriental villainess from his daily serial 'Terry and the Pirates': 'The Dragon Lady is everything a mortal could ask for. She occupies an honored wall in a frame which is everything she could ask for. For a lovely and a glamorous portrait of the loveliest and most glamorous personage in present-day fiction, my undying thanks. I wonder, though, what you can have, one half so precious as the stuff you draw. Gratefully and with sincerest admiration.' That Welles's fan letter is dated 1939, two years before he filmed Citizen Kane, suggests that he was an avid student of the strip.

Welles would have observed Caniff develop his signature illustration approach, starting with 'Terry and the Pirates' in 1934, and encouraged and

assisted by his brilliant studio colleague, Noel Sickles. Drawing in black and white for crude newsprint reproduction, Caniff broke away from conventional outlined cartoons and gave form to faces, figures, objects and settings out of his vibrant swathes and delicate delineations of black ink onto blank board. Their play of highlights and shadows, or 'chiaroscuro', often evoked the artificial lighting and high contrast in black-and-white films, a further example of the cross-pollination of ideas between film and comics. Even more striking to Welles might have been the dynamics of Caniff's visual storytelling and composition which exploded through the 1930s. As Austin Stevens wrote in 1979, 'Caniff's panels were so subtly planned that they looked like a storyboard for a movie to be produced ten years in the future. His use of extreme "camera angles", dramatic contrasts, the push and pull of a pictorial sequence, was paralleled only once during that period, and then in the very advanced movie Citizen Kane.'[2] Such 'subtle planning' was crucial to Welles too, who had his whole film drawn beforehand as a precise storyboard. It's no coincidence that storyboards superficially appear akin to comics. For their very first short silent film projected for an audience in Paris in 1895, the Lumière Brothers chose the simple visual skit of a gardener whose watering hose is blocked by a prankster stepping on it. Curious, the gardener looks closely at the nozzle and then, when the prankster releases his foot, he gets a drenching. The source of this gag was a one-page comic, of which there were several versions. Clear and concise, it made a perfect blueprint

One Soul
Ray Fawkes, 2011

from which to conceive and stage their film and was familiar enough with the public for them to understand the joke's actions and reactions.

As well as storyboards, comics can be said to resemble the sprocketed frames on a roll of film. Both are analagous with a fundamental element of comics, much more than the speech balloon, namely the strip. A row or tier of one or more panels, usually horizontal, sometimes vertical, the pictures forming a sequence, is the building block of the majority of comics. At their simplest, they are recognisable as the daily strips in newspapers, but they are also present in almost all comics pages, where they can be arranged together in larger configurations. Most readers know instinctively the order of strips, and therefore panels, and in what direction to read them across and down the page, one strip at a time, although

some early American Sunday newspaper pages, for example, would number the panels to avoid any confusion. In many Japanese comics, this legibility is reinforced by packing panels in strips more closely together horizontally and enlarging the blank spaces or gutters separating each strip, making each one almost like a frieze or printed screen. Widening the horizontal gap more between rows of panels in manga can be used to convey a change of scene. Out of these conglomerations of the basic strip have developed a wide range of layouts. Renaud Chavanne is one of several French-speaking theorists who have closely analysed the role of the strip as the primary structural unit in the layout of almost all comics, the underlying organising principle even where it is not so immediately obvious to the eye. Studying copious samples in *Composition de la bande dessinée* (2011), Chavanne distills five main types

ABOVE:
His Dream of Skyland, Vol.1
Anna Opotowsky (writer)
and Aya Morton (artist), 2011

RIGHT:
A Bride's Story
Kaori Moru, 2009

OVERLEAF:
George Sprott
Seth, 2009

being represented. In a fragmented layout, the height of the strip can be divided to form two or more shorter panels of variable heights or widths, multiplying further layout possibilities. Finally, Chavanne groups together other 'layouts in action', more or less complex, that move outside these first four categories.[3] Chavanne's system of analyses and filters permits us to see afresh the scaffolding and guidance system underpinning nearly all comics.

The American comics artist and theorist Scott McCloud, in *Understanding Comics*, placed emphasis on another property of the medium: 'closure', a hot-wired impulse in humans to forge some sort of meaning between one image and the next. Two panels juxtaposed seem to invite us to spot the difference and construct meaning, a before and after, a cause and effect. This leap of faith into the 'gutter' between panels, what the French more elegantly term the 'intericonic space', drives the reader onward through comics. Equally significant, however, is the reader's engagement with the whole page, its totality, and how it is organised and presented. Leafing through a comic or graphic novel, we have to understand the reading protocols, as Chavanne calls them, which guide how we will navigate the pages and their layouts. And before that, our first impression as we turn the pages is usually the double-page spread. Many comics creators are acutely aware of the impact they can achieve with the turning of the page. It is the only way to generate surprise or shock, because once the page is turned, our eyes inevitably glimpse

of layout. In a regular layout, the panels are of an unchanging, identical size, such as the three-by-three or nine-panel 'waffle' grid, used by Alan Moore and his collaborators in *Watchmen* and *From Hell*, or by Ray Fawkes in *One Soul* to chronicle eighteen lives in different eras, each occupying the same panel position across successive spreads (p.29). In a semi-regular layout, some regular panels may be split into two smaller panels, and others may be joined up to create larger ones. In a rhetorical layout, such as in *His Dream of Skyland*, (left), Anna Opotowsky and Aya Morton adapt and adjust the sizes and formats of panels to the demands of what is ahead. A peculiar discipline is needed as we read to narrow our focus onto just the first panel and then the next, and so on, restraining ourselves from discovering the punchline or twist lying ahead.

Another crucial system operating in comics is the persistence of images. Unlike the fleeting, flickering visuals of film or television, comics provide static, fixed images, which the reader can refer to again and again. Thierry Groensteen has proposed the principle of 'braiding' to describe how comics creators plant cues and clues, recurring motifs, symbols, colours, intended to spark recognition, memory, and other echoes through the story. Tapping into our urge to create patterns and observe links and relationships, braiding makes the medium highly interactive. Comics encourage, even demand, exploration and reflection, and scanning panels and pages permits readers to move easily back and forth through time.

In the remarkable climax of *George Sprott* by Seth (pp.32–3), the eponymous elderly Canadian broadcaster literally sees his life flash before his eyes as he dies from a heart attack. Seth has designed six pages to fold out from the graphic novel, compiling a mosaic of single photographs, short comics and a variety of graphic elements reminding us of what we have read so far and filling in the gaps and connections that make up this flawed, all-too-human protagonist. We are caught up in the intense synaptic undertow of his final moments, interrupted by insistent but unheard pleas from the real world to 'wake up'. It is the kind of audacious,

intense multiple moment, perceived all at once but readable slowly as we decode it, that is impossible in cinema or prose. Of course, readers of novels will retain memories of what they have read and can physically refer back to them, but with much less convenience than in a comic.

Debates over what essentially defines comics have gone beyond speech balloons or recurring characters and are being thrown wide open by such boundary-blurring variants as Posy Simmonds's textually enhanced *Gemma Bovery*, Brian Selznick's pure storytelling in pictures and in words in *The Invention of Hugo Cabret,* or Al Columbia's disturbing associative collage *Pim & Francie*. One property which comics share with some children's picture books or artist's books is the persistence of images, sometimes with text, on the page and how both creator and reader build these into a network of 'frames of reference', combining the persistence of vision with the persistence of memory. Reading a comic actively encourages re-reading, re-viewing, building up 'document literacy' of the whole narrative tapestry. This explains why Chris Ware has likened a comic to sheet music. A comic only truly comes alive when it is directed and animated in the reader's head. Because of this, each performance, each interpretation, each definition, will be unique.

MORE THAN WORDS CAN SAY:
SILENT COMICS

3

We can't help reading the city. In the modern metropolis, words are almost always vying for our attention, from newspaper headlines to advertisements, shop-fronts to road signs. To experience a world of wordlessness unmoors us from the familiar landscape of text. We have no choice but to step back into a pre-literate viewpoint – that of our young-child self or of our earliest ancestors – and rely on all our visual skills to make sense of the story around us. This visual literacy, or graphicacy, is one faculty fundamental to the understanding and enjoyment of comics. Nowhere is this more essential than in making sense of so-called 'silent' or 'pantomine' comics, those which make no use of speech or thought balloons, captions, or any text except perhaps for a title.

Any presence of words in comics immediately seems to impose a specificity and a duration, if only the time it takes the reader to read them. Shaun Tan has remarked on his decision to remove all words from his internationally acclaimed wordless graphic novel *The Arrival* (p.41): 'The moment you add words and captions, there's a real gravity. People look at them and they believe what the words are saying rather than interpreting them for themselves. That's a problem. Also it's got a set pace. Reading has a kind of kinetic flow. Pictures are more like a map. You can wander around them. There's not a line as such, a beginning, middle and end.'[1] Novice graphic novel readers coming from a prose novel background may undervalue or overlook those panels

or pages without words, always seeking the next reassuring, anchoring piece of text. It has been known for first-time readers of *Watchmen* by Alan Moore and Dave Gibbons to skip ahead, past several silent pages which open the book, to get to the next bit of writing, thereby missing some essential parts of the story. For some consumers of regular comics, it can come as a shock to discover an entire comic operating in pictures.

Many might assume that such comics would be mainly suited to tell the most basic of tales, pictorial primers ideal for the youngest of readers. Some of the greatest children's picture books, from Raymond Briggs's *The Snowman* to Mark Newgarden's *Bow Wow Bugs A Bug*, would seem to confirm that – until one looks more closely at their quiet sophistication. Admittedly, in some forms, especially short gags in strips of a few panels, a comic without words can be understood almost instantaneously. You have read it before you have time to decide not to read it. This immediacy explains their efficacy as information graphics such as airline safety manuals or instructional diagrams.

Late nineteenth-century Paris provided a bohemian, intellectual milieu for the development of these silent comics, when the Montmartre cabaret Le Chat Noir, founded in November 1881, began publishing them in its own magazine. While the content of these 'histoires sans paroles' was largely innocent, part of their adult appeal was to strip away serious, word-centered academia and recover our

Musical Competition. "A Lock of Your Hair, Maestro!" from Punch Almanack. 1894
Emmanuel Poiré ('Caran d'Ache'), 1893

— „ UNE MÈCHE DE VOS CHEVEUX, MAÈSTRO ! "....„

MUSICAL COMPETITION.

"A Lock of your Hair, Maëstro!"

inner child's ability to feel wonder at the most ordinary of phenomena. They also echoed the early experiments to make still images or photographs appear to move, as well as the silent shadow-puppet shows performed in the city's nightclubs. Appropriately, Théophile-Alexandre Steinlen, who designed the famous Chat Noir poster, let loose his black cat across a single page, delineating its feline antics.

Sharing these pages, Russian emigré cartoonist in Paris Emmanuel Poiré, whose pen-name Caran d'Ache was his French-style approximation of the Russian word for pencil, often told his short sequences in panels of the same size and from a fixed viewpoint and location. To maintain a seamless continuity, the shifts in time between pictures could be minute, moment-by-moment, encouraging the viewer to spot the differences from one picture to the next and imagine them almost moving. In fact, as Donald Ault has commented, 'Nothing moves in the process of reading a comic except our eyes and our imagination.'[2] In one strip of eight almost identical panels, Caran d'Ache contrasts the railway's rush of modernity with the languorous pace of the countryside by showing the slightest changes in a cow as it looks up to watch an unseen train travelling past, the cow's eyes and tail slowly moving, its mouth chewing, a farmer ploughing in the background, before it resumes its grazing.

This apparently simplest form of comics, however, is not always something slight, to be speed-read as if animating

a flip-book. The last twenty-five years or so have seen a plethora of silent comics emerge worldwide. This boom may be partly due to the influx of solo illustrators and animators into this field, sometimes primarily visual artists, who may be lacking in confidence in writing words or wary of having to incorporate them physically onto the same page and obscure or interrupt their image-making. In fact, far from being an easier option, making successful comics exclusively in pictures is highly challenging for creators, who can find themselves drawing many more panels to convey something that could be expressed with words much more concisely. This constraint therefore demands a high level of clarity and ingenuity, because they require more than might be expected in attention, concentration and interpretation from the reader. At their best, purely pictorial writing demonstrates a special property of comics to communicate succinctly and universally, transcending textual language barriers.

In recent years, the rich potential for a more extended narrative solely in images has been realised in several such longer-form graphic novels, but it was first seized upon more than a century ago. In 1894, Caran d'Ache wrote enthusiastically to the French newspaper *Le Figaro* proposing that they publish his innovative *roman dessiné*: 'On the inside, not a line of text! Everything will be expressed by drawings, about 360 pages of them.' He envisaged taking two or three months to produce *Maestro*, its provisional title, the tale of a musical prodigy,

The Idea
Frans Masereel, 1920

from humble village childhood to royal patronage and a global career. Shortsightedly, *Le Figaro* did not take up his offer of the first wordless 'drawn novel' and in 1909 whatever he had drawn of *Maestro* was sold off and scattered after the auction of his studio effects. His unrealised project vanished and remained a secret until it came to light in 1998 when the Museum of Comics in Angoulême, France acquired 108 of its inked pages. These were not consecutive and had pages missing. Subsequent discoveries have included four large notebooks containing over 140 sketches and ten folders of a synopsis, and a twenty-three-page synopsis handwritten in blue pencil, both in the Louvre's archives. More missing pieces of the puzzle keep coming to light; as recently as 2012 a 430-page preparatory dummy surfaced with hitherto unseen sequences drawn directly in ink. His notes on themes of wigs and baldness suggest that Caran d'Ache's 1893 single-page gag (p.35) about a virtuoso violinist, based on Ignacy Paderewski, may have partly prompted this project. Tantalisingly, other gaps may yet be filled, but it is already evident that this would have been a milestone in comics creativity.

Among Caran d'Ache's admirers was the British cartoonist H.M. Bateman, who wrote the introduction to the first posthumous collection of his work published in Britain in 1933, singling out his 'astounding observation and knowledge of humanity.'[3] Bateman's own pantomime strips are exemplars themselves, beginning innocently enough but escalating their theme to an absurd finale. Fellow cartoonist Ralph Steadman hailed Bateman's 'perfect emphasis of all good storytellers; I never feel that he put in even one frame too many. Every sequence is explained with consummate economy and the result is often filled with sadness and compassion, as you watch a character's life from birth to death enacted in so graphic a style.'[4] To do this requires much larger leaps in time, space and logic between panels than had been customary before. Bateman could condense a whole life story into a single page of thirty-one cartoons, from the arrest of 'The Boy Who Breathed on the Glass in the British Museum' through his trial, conviction and years in prison to his release and one final, elderly act of fatal defiance. Published mainly in the weekly magazine *Punch*, only a few of Bateman's comics were allowed to stretch beyond a page or two, but in 1923 the *Tatler* published his story 'Getting A Document Stamped at Somerset House' across four pages.[5] This Kafka-esque nightmare of bureaucracy follows one increasingly frustrated man battling through endless queues, stairs, corridors and misdirections, all for one essential stamp on his document. Bateman personally loathed the grasping tax office, so there's real anger behind his satire.

Another, altogether darker, more politically charged perspective, also stirring during the 1920s, finally generated the first extended silent comics, which looked more critically at the impact of larger forces on the individual. Deriving from printmaking training and traditions, their creators

avoided multiple images on a page, preferring to present a single, isolated image on the right-hand page of the spread, leaving the left blank. The sequence is still there, the reader can flick back and forth to build its connections, but two images are never seen together at once. That said, Dr Chris Mullen has pointed out that 'the previous illustration still registers a sort of memory presence through the paper', depending on the transparency of the stock and the heaviness of the inking.[6] An optimist and ardent pacifist, the Belgian Frans Masereel had his early novels in stark, angular, highly contrasted woodcuts published mainly in Germany. They include *Passionate Journey* (1919), charting one man's questing spirit in 165 images, and 1920's *The Idea* (p.37), portraying the power of an idea, symbolised as a muse-like woman, to resist and persist despite attempts by state, church and other vested interests to contain or change her.

Reflecting the more pessimistic times in Germany in 1926, Otto Nückel's bleak tale *Destiny* recounts through softer, more nuanced lead-cuts the tragic life of a young woman, portrayed mostly at a distance. On a more optimistic note, another much-loved German cartoonist in this genre was Erich Ohser who as 'e. o. plauen' began in 1934 drawing in crisp brushstrokes his endearing single-page vignettes between a father and a son, based on his relationship with his own son. Their first compilation sold 90,000 copies. The Nazis tried to co-opt Ohser's comics for propaganda purposes, though the Jewish artist refused to incorporate anti-Semitic messages. Arrested by the Gestapo on trumped-up defamation charges and facing deportation to a concentration camp, Ohser took his own life in 1944.

Masereel's influence would prove especially international and perennial, spreading as far as China, where an engraving movement of left-wing modernist artists sprang up. His work triggered the careers of America's pre-eminent pictorial novelist Lynd Ward and several current successors. It was while studying book design and printmaking in Leipzig in 1927 that Ward had an epiphany on discovering Masereel's work. Reading Nückel's novel *Destiny* in 1929 prompted Ward to set about producing his own. The longest and last of his six completed novels in wood engravings, *Vertigo* (p.39), published in 1937, was intended by him to be 'as explicit a statement as possible'. He combined three contrasting characters' perspectives and three different measures of passing time, in years, months and days. 'To accomplish that I broke down the action into many small steps, using several small blocks to bring the reader in close to a character so that facial expression would register more effectively the emotional response of that character to what was happening'.[7] In a compelling sequence, a sacked father attempts suicide so that his daughter can claim his life insurance.

Some might argue that Caran d'Ache or Bateman do not operate entirely without words, because they often rely on titles to foreground the story and prepare readers for the humour to

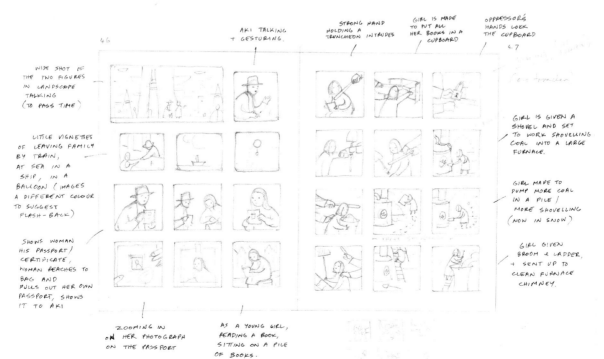

AKI TALKING
+ GESTURING.

STRONG HAND
HOLDING A
TRUNCHEON INTRUDES

GIRL IS MADE
TO PUT ALL
HER BOOKS IN A
CUPBOARD

OPPRESSORS
HANDS LOCK
THE CUPBOARD

46

47

WIDE SHOT OF
THE TWO FIGURES
IN LANDSCAPE
TALKING
(TO PASS TIME)

LITTLE VIGNETTES
OF LEAVING FAMILY
BY TRAIN,
AT SEA IN A
SHIP, IN A
BALLOON (IMAGES
A DIFFERENT COLOUR
TO SUGGEST
FLASH-BACK)

SHOWS WOMAN
HIS PASSPORT/
CERTIFICATE,
WOMAN REACHES TO
BAG AND
PULLS OUT HER OWN
PASSPORT, SHOWS
IT TO AKI

ZOOMING IN
ON HER PHOTOGRAPH
ON THE PASSPORT

AS A YOUNG GIRL,
READING A BOOK,
SITTING ON A PILE
OF BOOKS.
ANOTHER CHANGE OF
STYLE/COLOUR TO
SHOW A 'STORY WITHIN
A STORY!'

GIRL IS GIVEN A
SHOVEL AND SET
TO WORK SHOVELLING
COAL INTO A LARGE
FURNACE.

GIRL MADE TO
DUMP MORE COAL
IN A PILE/
MORE SHOVELLING
(NOW IN SNOW)

GIRL GIVEN
BROOM + LADDER,
+ SENT UP TO
CLEAN FURNACE
CHIMNEY.

come, whereas Masereel, Nückel and Ward provide only the most allusive of titles and rely on readers to make their own meanings. Art Spiegelman pinpoints 'the secret locked inside all wordless novels: the process of flipping pages back and forth, hunting for the salient details and labeling them, shakes the words loose to yield meaning. Wordless novels are *filled* with language, it just resides in the reader's head rather than on the page.'[8]

Wordless novels sold well and became something of a vogue for a time in America. Despite being published in the same week as the Great Crash in 1929, Ward's first, *God's Man*, would go on to sell over 20,000 copies over the next four years. But their earnestness was ripe for parody, so in 1930 American strip cartoonist and Charlie Chaplin collaborator Milt Gross sent them up, along with the hammy melodrama of silent movies, in *He Done Her Wrong*. Gross billed his 256-page farce as 'THE GREAT AMERICAN NOVEL and not a word in it – no music too', although to be accurate he did resort to signage, notably in a nifty two-page spread where the frontiersman hero is separated from his lady love and they narrowly miss finding each other thanks to a large, obstructing billboard of the word 'FATE'. With one or more images sprinkled across most pages, his book more closely resembles an unusually long, unravelled newspaper strip.

Wordless pictorial narratives persisted through the rise of the talkies in cinema, the massive success of the comic book 'all in color for a dime', and during and after the Second World War, albeit more intermittently. As an admirer of Don Freeman's 1955 book *Skitzy*, one day in the double life of Floyd W. Skitzafroid, half office worker, half artist, fellow Canadian cartoonist Seth noted: 'It seems that about every ten years in the early twentieth century somebody invented the graphic novel. Most of the time they seemed unaware of the previous attempts.'[9] There was some connection and continuity, for example, in the case of Laurence Hyde, who had corresponded with Lynd Ward before creating *Southern Cross* (1951) about the dire effects of atomic bomb tests on South Pacific islanders.

The most recent revival of silent comics seems to be building more solidly upon lessons of the past and sprang especially from the fields of children's books and radical alternative comics. English illustrator-turned-author Raymond Briggs began writing his own stories in 1973 about a grouchy Father Christmas. Restricted to the standard thirty-two-page unit of picture books for kids, Briggs had no choice but to subdivide pages to get his ideas across and so arrived at comics. In 1978, as light relief from two years' intense detail and verbal invention for *Fungus the Bogeyman*, he dusted off an earlier proposal, *The Snowman*, and produced an affecting classic. His variation of panel sizes and shapes here, larger ones to contain a longer passage of time or evoke the elevation and elation of flying, is subtly sophisticated.

Twenty-five years later, the discovery of Briggs's *Snowman* would offer

The System
Peter Kuper, 1997
Original artwork

42

Space Dog
Hendrik Dorgathen, 1993

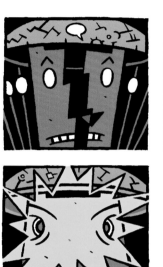

rented and none of appliances make any sense.' To do justice to these 'intimate, anecdotal tidbits' meant making *The Arrival* a longer book, 128 pages in all. Tan designed it as an artefact, like an old log-book or photograph album, with worn covers and sepia tones. Although he chose for the first time to use models and photo references, Tan was concerned when 'sometimes the drawings would look too realistic, too photographic, so I'd add lines so you can see that it's fake.'[10] Somehow drawings prove more believable and susceptible to interpretation.

Thematically, *The Arrival* harks back to Masereel's and Ward's empathy for the lost and dislocated in the threatening Big City. By creating a world both strange and strangely familiar, Tan enables us to share his immigrant's anxiety and wonder at his new home, his struggles with alien customs and languages, his encounters with other 'arrivals' from troubled lands, and his eventual sense of belonging. What better way could there be to do this than to remove all written language (Tan invents several plausible but indecipherable scripts for the book) and to force the reader to observe, deduce and adapt alongside his protagonist. Its international success proves that *The Arrival* works as a fable for anyone facing the challenges of life's changes.

When Peter Kuper and Seth Tobocman founded the magazine *World War 3 Illustrated* in 1980, the year of Ronald Reagan's election, they looked back to the heritage of political graphics that included Masereel. They invited Eric

direct encouragement to Australian children's book author Shaun Tan to pursue a wordless project about an immigrant's gradual adjustments to his baffling new home, *The Arrival* (p.41). 'The bit that fascinated me was where the snowman starts to be amazed by things like a detergent bottle, a refrigerator, a gas stove. For him this is all alien, domestic stuff and the boy takes great delight in showing him all these things. That was similar to a scene I'd thought of in my book where the immigrant first arrives in a room he's

Drooker to form a collective of artists and a home for outspoken comics with a radicalising message. In *The System* (p.43), Kuper taps into the iconic angularity of his predecessors to forge a signature style entirely suited to portraying present-day New York, using the street-art tools of stencils and coloured spray paints. He shows how a corrupt cop, a serial killer and a scheming politician are ensnared into an interconnected web of cause and effect in a pitiless city. Having been shown the books of Masereel and Ward by his grandfather, Drooker took up scraperboard to illustrate his urgent urban warnings, in *Flood! A Novel in Pictures* (1992) and *Blood Song: A Silent Ballad* (2002). Masereel also lives on in Andrzej Klimowski's linocut and photo-montage fables *The Depository* (1994) and *The Secret* (2002), adding dream-like metamorphoses and paranoia and reflecting his family background and art training in Poland.

The larger legacy of comics without words in Germany may partly explain why they have proved particularly vigorous there, notably since the country's reunification in 1990 spurred its independent publishing scene. Hendrik Dorgathen's *Space Dog* (pp.44–5) consciously echoes the Masereel tradition in his thick inky line-work and his story of the progress of an unnamed, wide-eyed farm dog who escapes to the city and ends up being trained by NASA. Rocketed into space, he meets aliens who enhance his intelligence and entrust him with a mission to save mankind from self-destruction. When Space Dog addresses the United Nations, everyone understands perfectly what he is saying, no matter what their mother tongue, because he speaks through icons placed around a globe inside his speech balloons. In the first, the aliens advocate enlightenment (an eyeball), solar energy (the sun and a cell), justice (scales) and love (a heart), whereas in the next, humanity's focus is on money (the dollar sign), nuclear fuel (a power station), injustice (a large foot chasing a tiny frightened figure) and death (a skull). Dorgathen employs bright flat colours, his square-headed dog standing out in red, and an arsenal of symbols to transmit feelings and meanings with crystal clarity.

There is a rugged, scratchy physicality to these Germanic storytellers' art. A fanciful, heart-shaped map of the warehouse district of Hamburg harbour becomes the prime location and character in Martin Tom Dieck's *One Hundred Views of the Speicherstadt* (1997). Pulsing through its whole-page images are ever-changing forms and bodies of water, seen from above and below, between canyons of docks and beneath tankers left high and dry. Mood and mystery are the goals here, rather than a single narrative. For Dieck, 'Words specify too much; only images know how to keep secrets.' The almost surgical scalpel incisions of Swiss-German Thomas Ott reveal slices of white and light from the blackness of his scraperboard pages, an apt medium with which to tell his visceral tales of the macabre. Another Swiss-German artist, Anna Sommer, cuts out shapes of coloured paper to build up her mischievous parables about the sexes.

'The tablecloth' from *L'Homme en pièces*
Marion Fayolle, 2011

Sommer is one influence on the young French artist Marion Fayolle, whose collection of fragmented silent narratives *L'Homme en pièces* (p.46) probes the tensions and strange secret desires in human relationships. Her barefoot characters, always shown head-to-toe, move across the page, empty except for the minimum of necessary props, like mute actors improvising on the most minimalist stage. Body language is the lingua franca here; one tilt of the head, one facial expression, one gesture or posture, can be as eloquent as pages of prose. There is an understated sensual charge to her vignettes, as women dive into the pool of wax left by a melted boyfriend or transform their long dresses into a tent or a table cloth for men to climb under. She also taps into myths and legends and gives them a witty twist, showing a son watered by his parents like a tree, only to grow so tall he devours his own father. Fayolle's cruel and amusing sequences echo the often dark humour and naturalistic draughtsmanship of Adolphe Willette, another of the *fin-de-siècle* Parisian artists who drew wordless sketches about the clownish Pierrot lovestruck by Colombine in *Le Chat Noir* magazine. Fayolle's manual processes of composing images by stamping areas of colour in a subdued, weathered palette also consciously hark back to earlier illustration.

The fragmentation of time in comics also enables us to freeze and meditate on fleeting events, deepening our appreciation of the ephemeral. British landscape printmaker Jon McNaught brings the mark-making and colour-mixing of traditional lithographs and relief prints to the medium, refining each borderless panel down to its sparsest elements and painstakingly drawing and separating by hand each layer of colour, typically black, grey, pale blue and sunset pink. In *Pebble Island* (right), he recaptures his wanderings as a boy on an island in the Falklands after the 1982 war, taking time to show the rain subsiding before he sets off cycling across the beach through shafts of sunlight. A sheep looks up and briefly watches him pass, like Caran d'Ache's cow over a century before.

Expanding time to one extreme, in *3"* (p.51), Marc-Antoine Mathieu has anatomised just three seconds into sixty-nine pages of nine square panels, each one continuously zooming into one object which reflects and reveals a new direction, character or detail. Uniquely, the reader looks out from inside a particle of light, bouncing from one shiny surface to the next, three seconds being all the time a photon needs to travel 900,000 kilometres from Earth to the moon and back, or for a bullet to reach its target. Like the slow-motion 'bullet time' in *The Matrix*, from these frozen vertiginous viewpoints of mere micro-moments we piece together a murder mystery about a sniper targeting an ex-footballer, a key witness in a match-fixing trial. Mathieu conceived this originally as digital animation which you can slow down and rewind, supplementing the analysis possible in print. Surely the shortest time-span of any graphic novel, *3"* is arresting for its fiendish construction and uncompromising experimentation.

Pebble Island
Jon McNaught, 2011

At the other temporal extreme, spanning millennia of mankind's development of language, John Miers explores the pictorial vocabulary of comics as a perfect metaphor for the origin of man's separation through a multiplicity of spoken tongues in his 2009 re-telling of the biblical tale of the Tower of Babel (pp.52–3). In the first of nine large prints reminiscent of illuminated manuscripts or stained glass windows, words become pictures filling speech balloons, as two speakers describe the sun, a tree, fire and water using identical images formed from those same objects behind them, thus representing the harmony of understanding between both speakers, and the exact resemblance between the description and the described object. Miers then shows language becoming more sophisticated, no longer based solely on observing nature but on man's discoveries as people unify to build the tower. To convey growing discord, Miers revisits his first print in the sixth and places differing, conflicting pictorial styles from works of art to represent the incompatible verbal languages which God, as an all-seeing eye, imposes on humanity. By the eighth, confusion reigns. Annotated with a Powerpoint presentation provided on CD or as a download, this suite stretches the communicative properties of textless comics to new levels.

In contrast to the babble of illustrated speech balloons, the constraint of silence in comics seems particularly effective in evoking dream-like states. The absence of all sound, the inability to hear or say anything, is puzzling,

even unnerving. This comes across in *Arzach* (1975), the quartet of fully painted fantasies by the French genius Moebius, which follow an enigmatic hooded rider and his pterodactyl through extraterrestrial landscapes. This same queasy quality can be found in Jim Woodring's *Frank*, a buck-toothed, white-gloved, willful critter resonant of America's early black-and-white animated cartoons, whose ongoing escapades can lurch from slapstick to atrocity in an instant. Woodring initially conceived Frank as speaking 'in a flowery, stylised dialect' or 'using so much profanity that it made my eyes feel grimy to read it', before realising that 'if I left the dialogue out entirely, it would reinforce the otherworldly mood of the story.' Woodring's visions are born of his waking dreams, hallucinations and intellect. His shimmering lines lend his picture stories a convincing heft and suggest a sort of ubiquitous, hypnotic hum. Far from being airy flights of fancy, his Frank universe asks difficult questions and taps into varied world folklores and pantheisms.

On the dustjacket of *Congress of the Animals* (2011), Woodring cites Sir Arthur Stanley Eddington from his book *Fundamental Theory* (1948), 'It seems to me that the first step in a broader revelation to man must be the awakening of image-building in connection with the higher faculties of his nature, so that these are no longer blind alleys, but open out into a spiritual world.' Silent comics can activate that instinctual image-building faculty, in the minds of their creator and their reader alike.

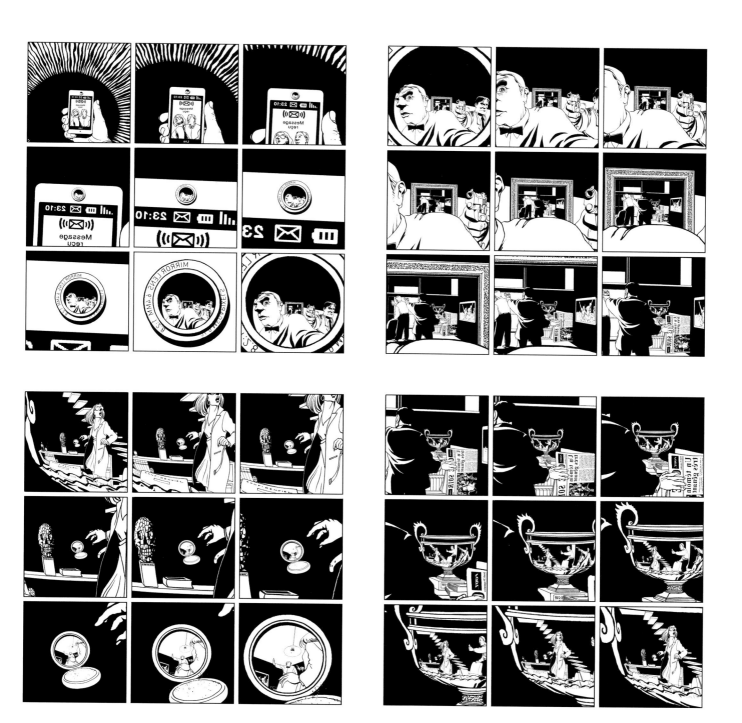

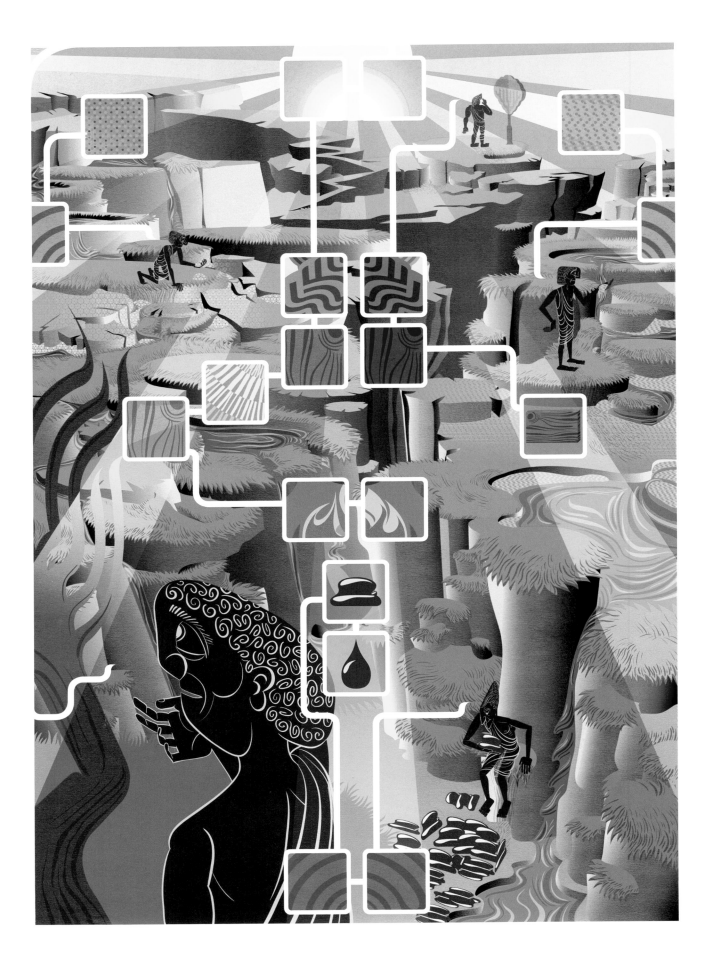

BETWEEN THE PANELS:
THE POWER OF THE PANEL

How long does a comic last? Unlike the audience's usual participation in such media as films or plays, with their more or less fixed duration in a cinema or theatre, how long we take to read a comic is entirely in our control. Makers of films are called directors, not only because they direct cast and crew and all involved in their making, but because they direct the viewer and the viewing experience. They can normally rely on the viewer's willingness to relinquish most, if not all, control to them, apart from the individual actions of shutting eyes, blocking ears or leaving the building. No wonder certain movies are likened to roller-coaster rides which you are strapped into and cannot get off. Perhaps when we watch a movie privately at home on DVD, online or in another format, we might choose to pause, slow down, re-wind or fast-forward, but aside from these digital interventions, most of us watch a film or play unfold before us in its own time, the director's pre-set time.

A comic doesn't come with a running time. To read all the words without recourse to the images requires a certain length of time, as in a prose book. But as we've seen when you exclude all text, far from being quicker and easier, wordless comics can be demanding and more like puzzles. Without or with words, the drawings themselves require attention and comprehension and this time is less easily quantified.

There is a contradictory tension in making and reading comics. On the one hand, the comics creator wants to slow the reader down so they pick up all the relevant narrative content, visual as well as verbal, contained in each panel. On the other hand, the creator also wants to motivate the reader to leave that panel and move on to the next. The 'directors' of comics have tools and techniques to achieve both of these goals, guiding the 'eye stream' by structuring images and placing texts to flow across the page, but they can only do so much to direct the independent reader. Rather than a weakness of the comics medium, it is a strength. In contrast to the manipulative tools of moving images that can hold an audience in thrall, comics are modest in scale and means and have to work much harder without sound, motion, music and emoting, photogenic actors. If comics mostly are 'It's only lines on paper, folks!', as Robert Crumb once quipped, it is a wonder that they should work at all and make us feel and care about them.

Perhaps there is always a distance, a remove, no matter how much we suspend disbelief, but at their best, comics draw you in. Shaun Tan has commented on one way to do this by keeping his stories half-finished and considering his readers as his co-creators. 'Above and beyond any simple story or "message", I believe that the personal reflections of the reader are far more important than those of an author ... My own practice ... really just involves crafting a *space* in which the thoughts of another person can flourish, especially in ways that are impossible to conceive until you actually start reading, writing, or drawing.'[1]

Jimmy Corrigan, The Smartest Kid on Earth
Chris Ware, 2000

The choice of pictures and words inside a panel are important, but equally so are the proportion, location and relationship of that panel to other panels in its immediate vicinity and as part of the whole page or 'multiframe', as well as on the double-page spread and more generally within the story or book as a whole (the 'hyperframe'). From preparing the first sketches, layouts and scripts, there are certain protocols which the 'comics director' typically tries to resolve and propose, among them which uniform grid or multiple grids will determine how panels will be arranged on the page. This preliminary is of course predetermined partly by the format of the finished comics, but within those parameters lie a fertile range of options to create pacing, moods or contrasts. Similarly, before beginning a comic, an alert reader will assess and acclimatise to these panelling protocols, among others, and adjust to their specific effects. It is all part of the process of pattern recognition that readers bring to all comics.

In 1953, the author George Mikes wrote anonymously in the *Times Literary Supplement* about his misgivings over the growth of comics and lamented their shortage of room for proper draughtsmanship. 'It was always extremely difficult to draw well in the small squares in which the balloons occupied a large part of even that limited space. The best the more able artists could do was to give evidence of the fact that they could draw better in more fortunate circumstances.'[2] While it is true that comics have rarely operated at the same impressive

grandeur as paintings made for the walls of art galleries or stately residences or films on huge cinema screens, refined arresting artistry is not necessarily the aim of images in comics. Panels are not always restrictive, or indeed always of the same proportions. No matter how Cinerama-widescreen or IMAX-scale a cinema screen becomes, a movie as it is projected tends to conform to that format and remain unchanged. One property peculiar to comics is that a panel can vary as much as the readability, paper dimensions and any other adjacent panels allow.

Size really does matter in comics, not just because of how much or how little you can fit within a panel, but because it is the medium where time equals space. As a broad rule, smaller panels tend to represent smaller amounts of time and so can be ideal for conveying a process or a more rapid succession of events close together in time. Jim Steranko, a unique example of a complete writer-artist working at Marvel Comics in 1968, opened the first issue of *Nick Fury Agent of S.H.I.E.L.D.* with four pages of uniform narrow panels in two tiers of four showing the secret agent's break-in to a supervillain's lair. Their wordlessness reinforces Fury's undetected stealth and their regulated pacing seems to underline the hero's cool methodology. An oddity at the time, Steranko's silent pages almost went unpaid because of management's objections that he had not written any text, and hence any story.

Smaller panels can also be added to project psychological states, for example in Joe Sacco's *Palestine*, where the effects of torture and confinement on a prisoner are reflected in the pages' increasingly reduced, oppressive panel sizes. Here, the black background between the panels only adds to the sense of claustrophobia. A shortage of pages for his story forced Raymond Briggs to squeeze his elderly couple in *When The Wind Blows* into up to thirty panels per page, but this only underlined their small domestic world and their constrained circumstances, as they struggle to survive a nuclear attack. Another effect is produced by the repetitious, cramped squares of Mark Newgarden's *Pud + Spud*, straining the reader's eyeballs and patience with their stupid and sad existences. Reducing the characters to slight marks for big noses and grins emphasises their limited existences, their limited world.

The same sort of density is used by confessional cartoonists Joe Matt and David Heatley to pack their pages with small panels, up to forty-eight in Heatley's case, as many as sixty-six by Matt, all on one page. It's no surprise that Matt has admitted: 'I sort of feel compelled to write about every sexual encounter.'[3] Both artists cram their comics to relate their unexpurgated experiences, creating an intensity of frankness, an outlet for getting a lot off their chest, unable to prioritise and giving everything equal importance and so equal size. Choosing small panels can defuse potential sensationalism, as in Chester Brown's autobiographical graphic novel *Paying For It* about his relationships with prostitutes, which sets out not to arouse but to

work as a matter-of-fact reportage. Perhaps the most exaggerated use of minute panels is *Longshot Comics*, in which Shane Simmons overcomes his modest drawing skills by showing all his characters at extreme distance as nothing more than dots and relating his entire story in 3,840 longshots.

Introducing reduced panels can also produce intriguing effects. For his two-page exercise from 1980, 'The Plot Thickens' (pp.58–9), Bill Griffith tries the constructional conceit of adding one panel to each row across the page to complicate the story incrementally while the available space shrinks smaller and smaller. Griffith opens on a full-width panel of his principal character Charles Bendix, sitting in a spacious cafe, his circumstances explained in a sixty-two-word caption. Diagonal striped borders suggest a crime scene or border crossing, rows of dots suggest ticker tape and the lines dividing the captions suggest a ruled notebook. Griffith then progresses down the two pages adjusting from two panels across, then three, then four, getting shorter and smaller each time. He winds up in the eleventh row with eleven miniscule panels, their captions devoid of verbs, their images unable to fit speech balloons, their content mere snatches of the people or objects described, ending full circle with the elusive spoon which Charlie Bendix was wishing for when his tale began. A spoon barely able to stir this thickening, congealing, imploding plot.

In contrast to Griffith's absurdist experiment, other artists introduce

OVERLEAF:
'The Plot Thickens', from Raw Vol.1, No.2
Bill Griffith, 1980

THE PLOT THICKENS

IT WAS A COLD, CLEAR AFTERNOON. CHARLIE BENDIX STIRRED HIS COFFEE WITH A FINGER AS HE CONTEMPLATED HIS NEXT MOVE. THE CAFETERIA WAS EMPTY. IN FACT, IN THAT VAST CAVERN OF TABLES AND CHAIRS, CHARLIE WAS THE ONLY THING STIR RING. THERE WAS NOTHING IN THE PAPER. CHARLIE BENDIX WAS 36. HE STIRRED HIS COFFEE WITH A FINGER AND HE SAID TO HIMSELF

THEN SHE CAME INTO HIS LIFE. SHE WAS A REPORTER FOR A BIG CITY NEWSPAPER. ON THE SIDE SHE DID "NEON SCULPTURE". SHE LOVED CATS. SHE LOVED DOGS. SHE LOVED PIZZA & SHE LOVED CHARLIE BENDIX.

TEXAS WAS ALIEN TO CHARLIE. HE MISSED THE OCEAN... HE DIDN'T LIKE COWBOY HATS. HE DIDN'T LIKE LONE STAR BEER. HE DIDN'T LIKE THE WIDE, OPEN SPACES. AND HE DIDN'T LIKE LESTER

LESTER MISTOOK CHARLIE'S DEFERENCE FOR FRIENDSHIP. CHARLIE MARRIED SHIRLEY. THEN ONE DAY:

CHARLIE MISTOOK LESTER'S HOSTILITY FOR PATHOS. HE RELATED AN INCIDENT FROM HIS PAST.

ACTUALLY, CHARLIE WAS LYING. IT WAS HIS 2 YEAR THE PRIESTHOOD THAT LED HIM TO THE THE CRAPS TA

Valentina: Annette
Guido Crepax, 1972

heroine Valentina working on a shoot, another the photographs she is taking, like a roll of film or a print of four passport photos. Crepax also mixed in tight close-ups, perhaps of a face or a fingertip's touch, to capture his lovers erotic charge and heightened senses.

At the other extreme of the scale of panels, when the whole page or a double-page spread becomes one single image, it suggests not only a larger space but a larger time, inviting the reader to linger and lose themselves. Jack Kirby championed the large single image in American comic books starting in the 1940s. He employed them more consistently in his stories starting in the 1970s, which he would regularly open with an explosive two-page action scene or expansive vista, thrusting the reader *in media res*. During this period, Philippe Druillet in France worked on unusually large artboards to compose his fantastical tableaux of cyclopean architecture and tumultuous battlefields, while Steranko upped the game in *Nick Fury* by crafting the first panoramic panel to stretch across four consecutive pages, requiring readers to buy two copies of the comic book to view the whole spectacle.

Impact is one result of these methods, but so too is immersion. This is especially true in manga or Japanese comics when a two-page image is allowed to bleed off the outer edges of the pages. The readers' frames of reference are gone; there are no borders. Not only does this suggest that what we can see is only part of an even bigger place continuing beyond the physical

reduced panels to heighten awareness of the present. Chris Ware has found the insertion of clusters of same-sized square panels, dividing the regular panel height in two, a highly effective way to present transitions or actions, often quite minimal and from a fixed viewpoint, akin to miniature animations. Ware unfolds a moment's respite (p.55): a door closing, snow crunching, a passing truck, birdsong, shivers, cold breath.

Similarly, before Ware, 1960s Italian innovator Guido Crepax would weave little panels or sequences within his layouts to record subtle moments and movements (above). One vertical row of four panels might show his

William Shakespeare's Hamlet
Raoul Traverso ('Sigma') (writer) and Gianni de Luca (artist) 1975

paper, it also translates into a temporal expansion, expressing a larger moment in time. The turning of a page is the only way to surprise the reader of a comic, because unless we are unusually self-disciplined, our gaze cannot avoid looking across the immediate spread to scope out what lies ahead. Chancing upon a 'bleed spread' in manga is arresting. There is only one image to read, filling our field of vision, with nothing else vying for our attention. Our pace of reading, the time we allocate for each page, and our normal process of closure between panels are all disrupted. We have no choice but to be present.

Applied judiciously, this effect can prove striking. In *Children of the Sea*, for example, Daisuke Igarashi catches us unawares when he suddenly plunges us into the ocean depths and we swim ecstatically alongside his uncannily evolved merboys. Kazuo Umezu hammers home the shock of the headmaster's injury in *The Drifting Classroom* by showing it not once but in three spreads from different angles,

ending with a close-up of his bleeding head. Unlike in manga, for some reason publishing and printing conventions in the West have seldom permitted images in comics to bleed and escape both their frames and the page's surrounding outer border of blank paper. Thanks largely to the influence of manga, this technique has now become accepted, and so ubiquitous in much of the American superhero genre that its distinct effects have been diminished. Far more effective is Raymond Briggs's limited use in *When The Wind Blows*, when he suddenly cuts away to the approaching bomber planes and lets an entire spread dissolve to the blinding brilliance of the bomb exploding. Briggs strips the page clean to expose the white of the paper itself.

Double- and whole-page panels have rarely been constructed and choreographed so skilfully as in Gianni de Luca and Raoul Traverso's visualisation of Shakespeare's *Hamlet* in 1975 (above), in which he turns almost all the forty-eight pages into remarkable theatrical sets, through which his actors move, speak and perform, reappearing multiple times. Across one spread, at midnight, the Danish prince is repeated ten times as he enters on the left and walks along the battlements, joining Horatio, who then alerts him to his father's ghost who appears twice on the right-hand side, floating, as the pair of men, shown seven times in all, hurry to follow him. Hamlet's soliloquy is masterfully captured by showing him sixteen times, like some Eadweard Muybridge motion-study photograph, entering the room from back left and circling pensively, before stepping towards us to speak and exit bottom left. De Luca transforms the page into the stage, open and spacious, mostly unfettered by panels. Beyond the huge demands of composition and sheer draughtsmanship this entails, de Luca always maintains a path for readers to follow that is totally free of confusion. In its online exhibition *La BD avant la BD*, the Bibliothèque nationale de France highlights this repetition technique in a fourteenth-century manuscript of the *Roman de la Rose*, describing it as 'cinétique du déplacement' (kinetic displacement) and crediting de Luca for its reinvention. The 'de Luca effect' is so challenging that other comics artists have rarely attempted it so consistently. At best, they have used it for the occasional 'party piece'. Frank King, for example, drew a set of 'Gasoline Alley' Sunday newspaper strips in 1934 showing children playing around a building site as a house is constructed week by week, the whole scene subdivided into twelve panels, while Frank Miller

and Lynn Varley devoted one full-page panel in *Elektra Lives Again* (1990) to showing Matt Murdock waking from a nightmare and then seven consecutive versions of him getting dressed as he descends a staircase.

As discussed above, different amounts of time can transpire within panels, big or small. Sometimes as we read and scan across a panel, both the question and the response, or the cause and effect, can occur within the same one panel. Within that area, time becomes space, elastic and mutable, and the most ephemeral instant can expand into a whole lifetime flashing before your eyes. With narratives comprised of fixed images, comics art is a medium like no other in enabling us to observe past, present and future simultaneously and permanently and to move freely around inside the pages, time-travelling as we turn the leaves forwards and backwards, holding a life in our hands. Where else can we be offered such an overview of both the passage and synchronicity of time? This is one of ways in which comics seem to embody our associative, fluid thought processes, whereby at any moment our thinking, our attention, can be in the present, the past and the future. Flicking back and forth through the pages, it all becomes the now.

Even more flexible and unquantifiable than the time within each panel is the time that passes between them. In his essay 'Librorum Comicorum Explicatio' (Explanation of Comic Books), Donald Ault proposes: 'Comics attempt to depict forms of process in static slices of that process, each frame pointing beyond

**'Tomorrow You Live, Tonight I Die'
from Captain America 112**
Jim Steranko, March 1969

itself in two directions, becoming a momentary focus in the continuous flow of "reality". The comic artist controls the extent to which the reader has to fill the gaps between frames, and the reader's freedom to do so. Each frame is limited and suggestive: our feeling of the "reality" of our experience inheres as much in the voids between frames as it does in the drawings themselves. Each frame limits our perception and opens new possibilities: as we perceive each successive frame we reevaluate prior frames and anticipate those to follow.'[4] That gap or 'gutter' seems to be both a peculiar in-between space, liminal, and an unconscious space, subliminal. Whether it is a thin

empty space, or merely a single dividing line, or even just enough blank space to separate one floating, unframed panel from the next, each one resembles a blink of the eye, a tiny blackout, a temporal and/or locational hiatus, a blank canvas onto which our intuition and imagination can project. As much as Ault suggests that the comicS artist 'controls' how much and how freely the reader bridges from one panel to the next, it is hard to prevent a reader making highly personal associations and connections which are impossible to anticipate. Readers have been known to recall scenes not portrayed on the page but implied between the panels, which they have vividly imagined. This is another reason why there is more to comics than meets the eye.

Central to the idea is Ault's observation that each frame points not only forwards but also backwards. As we've already seen, reading comics is not merely a constant forward progress, an unfolding of one frame after another, a joining up of the dots. This is why dissecting pages of comics into separate panels to fit one at a time onto the small screen of a mobile phone so often dissolves their vital multi-linear interconnectivity. McCloud's *Understanding Comics* stresses closure (see p.30), while Will Eisner's term 'sequential art' prioritises sequence, but the process of making and reading comics is not one-directional. In the prologue to *George Sprott*, Seth portrays the floating heads of his character morphing from an unborn baby to a dead old man and back again, presumably floating in some pre-natal state and some afterlife, perhaps one and the same space, very much like the space between the panels, as they comment on this very feature. The ruminations of Sprott the younger and Sprott the elder begin with his questioning of an Inuit elder who provides a metaphor for the way he can foresee the future: 'It's like the stitches in this seal skin. It's all there to be seen. The stitch before and the stitch after decide the shape of middle stitch.' It's only later, 'while reading the funny pages', that Sprott comes to understand this. 'Maybe it's like these funnies? ... These boxes in a row ... perhaps they're not just a sequence. Perhaps the action in the middle box ... isn't merely determined by the action in the box before it. Maybe it is also influenced by what must occur in the box that follows. It needs to fulfil and anticipate in both directions. Maybe it is in this way that the future determines the present as much as the past.'

The reading order of panels is normally obvious enough, from top to bottom, from left-to-right, or, for example in manga, right-to-left, although in several cases during the nineteenth and early twentieth centuries, cartoonists felt it necessary to number the panels, fearing that novice readers would otherwise lose their way. As comics became a more widespread and understood medium, numbering became less necessary. It can be argued that it is a weakness of page layout if a comic artist is obliged to indicate the order of panels, for example with an arrow. In his 1975 experiment 'A Day at the Circuits', Art Spiegelman sets out to interfere with the regular reading

order by deliberately using arrows to re-direct the reader on counterintuitive paths, turning his single page of eleven panels about a depressed alcoholic and his drinking companion into a maelstrom of multiple strips. The page contains never-ending cycles – including their circular conversation and bouts of boozing – of seven, four, or as few as two panels, with others finite and converging on a dead end. Chris Ware has shamelessly added arrows to his more complex layouts in *Building Stories* (2012) to guide the reader. A sustained rethinking of the reading order of panels, drawn in 1996 and 1997, informs Brian Chippendale's *Maggots* (right), whose 344 pages try out a boustrephodon or zig-zagging system, only making some sense if you read alternately left-to-right, then on the next row right-to-left, snaking down the left-hand page and then up again on the right-hand page. More storytelling than story, Chippendale blurs diary and fantasy in his unstructured, momentum-driven unravelling, like the free-wheeling, open-ended play of a video game.

By avoiding clear, aligned sequences of panels, some comics artists have deliberately sought to create an orderless page. What can this produce? The mainly non-sequential panels in Steranko's opening page to *Captain America* 112 (p.63) combine to convey the gaudy penny-arcade location and mounting tension through the images and signage of a shooting gallery, stiletto blades and staring dolls as prizes. Woven through the page, though, is a three-panel sequence of

Maggots
Brian Chippendale, 2007

RIGHT:
Dr Spitzner's Wax Museum
François Rivière (writer) and Andreas Martens
('Andreas') (artist), 1978

BELOW:
Everything We Miss
Luke Pearson, 2011

a gypsy fortune-telling automaton dispensing its deadly prediction.

On one page of his medical thriller *Ode to Kirihito* (1970–1), Osamu Tezuka creates a peculiar irregular composition, like four vertical film-strips reading top to bottom. It is soon evident, however, that there is no one correct reading sequence, but a cumulative effect of the man struggling and straining as he transforms into a beast beneath

his woollen headgear. The fourth strip, containing the most panels (eight in all), starts, or ends, with the man's head completely reversed and upside down. The middle two strips can be read separately but the panels align precisely near the middle, suggesting they can be read in two circular cycles. Tezuka places this opposite a startling whole-page image of swirling, contorted bodies, a homage to Utagawa Kuniyoshi's *ukiyo-e* print of entangled male wrestlers, a

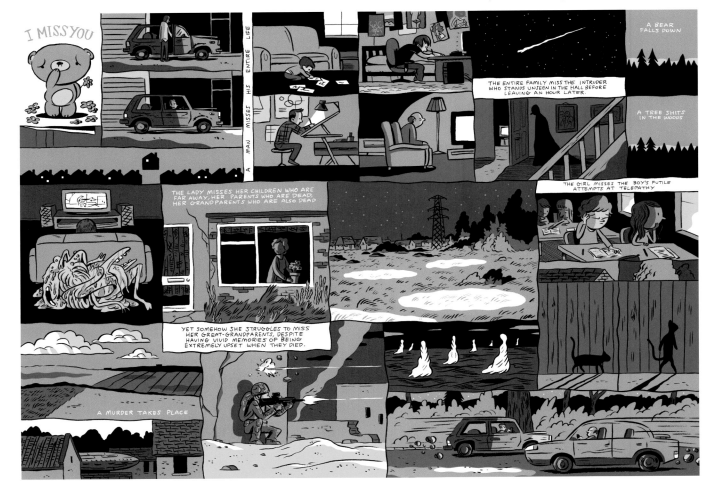

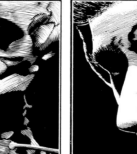

Et soudain, je la vis ! Elle était là, derrière un rideau que j'avais machinalement écarté. Elle reposait sous un panneau vitré et sa poitrine, lentement, régulièrement, se soulevait...

Ses yeux de porcelaine, son sourire de madone eurent sur mon système nerveux l'effet de la foudre ! Dès cet instant, je fus incapable de me contrôler: je croyais la reconnaître, elle vivait, c'était sûr et son corps palpitant, à demi dénudé, m'appelait de toutes ses fibres...

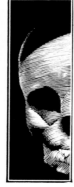

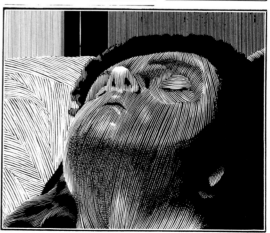

iconic image recognisable to many Japanese readers, and a mirroring of the entangled contents of the facing panels.

A similar moment of mental overload appears in 'Dr Spitzner's Wax Museum' by François Rivière and Andreas (p.67), where the narrator first encounters the uncannily realistic wax woman, 'her breast slowly, regularly respiring …' There is an opening and closing of sorts in the man's startled glance and the woman's head, eyes shut, but all the other panels surround the central caption in a kaleidoscope of disjointed fragments, glimpses of horrors, eyes and eye sockets, living, dead and artificial, essentially experienced and understood as simultaneous. In *Everything We Miss* (p.66), Luke Pearson fills one spread beyond capacity with overlapping panels presenting a multitude of phenomena in his world where the extraordinary takes place everyday, just out of view, unnoticed.

The possibilities of containing more than one time zone within one panel were radically expanded by Richard McGuire in his influential 1989 masterwork 'Here' (right).[5] Moving into a new apartment, McGuire was planning to try a split-screen effect on his comics assignment for his class with Art Spiegelman and began imagining all the people who had called the place home before him. From this spark, he chose to draw the echoes of lives past and future from the constant view of one non-descript corner of a room, anchoring us in space. By overlaying or 'encrusting' smaller vignettes captioned with their dates within the regular

panel composition, he can range non-sequentially, increasingly far and wide in time. He starts sedately from one initial year, 1957, appropriately the year of his birth, before clipping the edges of the scene of his mother sitting with the baby, freeing space to surround it with the same room in 1922, home to a pair of flappers. Next, cropping the 1957 maternal scene still more, he shows a swinging chick from 1971 and a black cat from 1999, who proceeds to walk, wash and leave – how much time this takes is left to us to imagine. Glimpses of McGuire's alter-ego's life so far and his possible life and death to come accumulate. With the information we glean from each new or repeated year, we're invited to make connections to what has gone before or lies ahead, such as the inset animals from 1860 revealing the location's former existence as a farm. Snapshots through centuries, from the dawn of Earth to forty years into the future of a fire in 2029 that foreshadows the building's demolition, entwine with mere seconds of a glass dropping or a mouse-trap snapping, or years of interminable housework.

A playful yet serious designer-polymath, McGuire is working on expanding his premise into a 300-page graphic novel, focusing on another corner of a living room, this one in his old family home, apparently the site of several historically significant events. In McGuire's hands, comics demonstrate some of their unique properties. Seldom has the relativity of time and of our own place within it been expressed so elegantly or emotionally. The real wonder is that any of us are 'here' at all.

Here
Richard McGuire, 1989
Original artwork

UNHEARD VOICES:
WHO IS AFRAID OF COMICS?

**'Ode to Harvey Kurtzman', from
Harvey Kurtzman's Strange Adventures**
Robert Crumb, 1989

Comics are usually made to sell. They have been a hugely lucrative form of entertainment, not always benefiting their creators as much as their corporate copyright owners. Whenever their products are intended to appeal to a mass market, comics creators can be susceptible to pressures, both external and internal to their creation, which almost inevitably shape the kinds of stories and art offered to the public and determine whose voices we hear, and consequently whose we do not. Rooted in ancient myths and continued in modern icons like Tarzan or Superman, certain heteronormative ideals such as the handsome, strong male lead and his beautiful but subsidiary female love interest are offered up again and again, with variations or revisions, as archetypes of wish-fulfilment presumably still popular and reassuring to enough people to prove commercial. Fortunately, there are many other comics, more so today than ever, that suggest that anyone can be the hero, or the heroine, of their own stories and their own lives.

Tensions between conformity and rebellion, commercialism and personal expression, have been rife in comics. Pressures on creators can come from publishers and editors eager to conform to the status quo or a proven formula; they can also be caused by censorship, perhaps prompted by the campaigns of self-appointed moral guardians and media scare-mongers, or from publishers' in-house rules or even enshrined as official legislation. More subtly pernicious is the need some writers and artists feel to censor themselves, most commonly to appease their employers and keep their jobs, which can result in the more private and political messages that conflict with established order being watered down or excised altogether.

That said, although labouring more than most media under the mistaken assumption that they should cater solely for children, comics are essentially no more compromised than films or television in their resistance to accommodate unconventional ideas. We have already seen in Hearst's support of a lifetime contract for Herriman to produce 'Krazy Kat', and in the powerful wordless novels of Masereel, Ward and their successors, that there have been creators, and publishers too, who are so committed that they will put aside their money-making self-interest to spread their convictions to a wider readership. Similarly, around the turn of the twentieth century, America's nascent, unregulated newspaper strips could be at their most raucous, free-wheeling and disrespectful when they addressed a very broad public, often working-class, immigrant, new to the culture and not necessarily fully literate in English. Not surprisingly, the potential of this populist proletarian literature to inspire discontent, even rebellion, among the masses gave cause for alarm among those in authority. The fact that the 'Funnies' appeared in the Sunday papers was enough to offend many of the devout, while other arbiters of taste lamented their vulgarity.

Sensitive to such criticisms, American publishers softened their strips in the

ODE TO HARVEY KURTZ

by R. CRUMB

©1989

I REMEMBER WHEN I SAW THE FIRST ISSUE OF **MAD** IN A MAGAZINE STORE, OCTOBER, 1952... I WAS NINE YEARS OLD... IT MADE A DEEP IMPRESSION...

WHA-A-?

"IT'S MELVIN"??

??

I'M NOT READY FOR THIS!

A YEAR OR TWO PASSED... I GREW OLDER... THE COVER OF MAD #11 CHANGED THE WAY I SAW THE WORLD FOREVER!

THIS LOOKS JUST LIKE *LIFE* MAGAZINE, ONLY — ONLY —

FROM THEN ON I READ MAD REGULARLY, BUT ONLY IN THE STORE... BRINGING A COPY HOME WAS UNTHINKABLE...

"MICKEY RODENT"!

TA HA HA HA

HEY, YOU GONNA BUY THAT FUNNY BOOK?

AFTER **MAD** TURNED INTO A MAGAZINE IT WAS HARD TO FIND AND I LOST TRACK OF IT, BUT THEN ONE DAY IN 1957 AT THE LOCAL SODA SHOP I SAW HUMBUG #2 SITTING IN THE MAGAZINE RACK.

WHAT IS THAT?!

THAT COVER WAS THE HEAVIEST CULTURAL ARTIFACT I HAD EVER SEEN! I WAS *SENT*!!

DING DONG

FROM THAT MOMENT I BECAME A RABID FAN OF HARVEY KURTZMAN... I *LIVED, BREATHED* AND *ATE* THE PAGES OF HIS MAGAZINES.... I WAS TRULY IN *LOVE*!!

WHAT ARTWORK!

WHAT A VISION OF AMERICA!

I HAD TO HAVE THEM ALL... I ROAMED THE ALLEYS LOOKING IN TRASH CANS FOR OLD ISSUES FROM 1955 & '56... THEM THINGS WERE DOGGONE HARD TO FIND!

OH, I MUST HAVE MADS 24, 26, 27 & 28 !!

I HAD DREAMS OF IMAGINARY ISSUES OF **MAD** MAGAZINES I WAS MISSING!

OBOY! MINE ALL MINE!

1920s to target more affluent middle-class readers, above all so that they could sell advertising space in their newspapers to national companies, a source of revenue which became much more significant than sales of the papers on newsstands or through subscriptions. Symptomatic of this makeover was Outcault's success with a follow up to 'The Yellow Kid' in the much more domesticated imp in Little Lord Fauntleroy clothes, 'Buster Brown'. Every Sunday, this milder mischief-maker regularly wound up learning his lesson in proper behaviour and signing a wordy, worthy resolution which filled the final panel. Less explicitly moralising messages than this are generally revealed on closer reading within most comics, even the most apparently anodyne. 'Buster Brown' was only one of many American strips which were clearly aspirational and promoted consumerism to readers. Their efficacy at conveying messages and values made comics vital in the wars of propaganda, demonising the enemy into something subhuman while extolling patriotic zeal. After 1945, for example, the American forces occupying Japan cleverly chose to translate into Japanese the family comedy strip 'Blondie' to help inculcate its idealised suburban lifestyle, the woman as mother, housewife and shopper, and so motivate the populace's productivity and spending.

Their very efficacy also gives comics a troubling reputation. After the Second World War, governments bowed to pressure and enacted legislation to ban what were perceived as offensive American comic books in France and Canada in 1949 and in Britain in 1955. To this day, cycles of moralising panics about the corrupting influence of comics have been stoked in various countries. Most recently, the 'invasion' of manga has sparked complaints and bans abroad, while in July 2011 the Tokyo Metropolitan Government expanded its restrictions on sales or rentals of comics and animation to people under the age of 18 to materials it considers 'to be excessively disruptive of social order.' What makes the authorities so anxious about this sequential storytelling? Michael Demson and Heather Brown suggest in part that 'To appeal to a broader audience, comics celebrate unruliness; they tend to promote caricatures scathing of those in authority while at the same time sympathetic to the disenfranchised; and, they propagate a lower-class vernacular that is immediately accessible. These features strengthen the sociability of comic readers.'[1] What lies behind much of the alarmist hyperbole against comics from conservative lobbyists and officials has always been the medium's power to communicate unacceptable ideas to the 'wrong' sort of people.

One example of the unifying and radicalising effect which certain comics can have on their readers is the original *Mad* comic books started by Harvey Kurtzman at EC Comics, New York in 1952. Among the impressionable youths hooked on the satirical *Mad* were Robert Crumb (p.71), Gilbert Shelton, Art Spiegelman and the majority of the American cartoonists who would transform the medium a decade or so later in underground comics for

adults. *Mad*'s impact went beyond comics. According to Spiegelman, '*Mad* was an urban junk collage that said "Pay attention! The mass media are lying to you ... including this comic book!" I think Harvey's *Mad* was more important than pot and LSD in shaping the generation that protested the Vietnam war.'[2] Cultural historian Steven Heller went further, hailing Kurtzman as 'the spiritual father of postwar American satire and the godfather of late-twentieth-century alternative humour.'[3] In turn, after *Mad*, the American underground comix (the 'x' for X-rated) went on to have a liberating effect on their readers and creators-to-be, at home and abroad.

In that tradition, another example is *Metro*, the first adult graphic novel published in Egypt in 2008, whose creator, Magdy El Shafee, and publisher were put on trial and eventually fined, their book being outlawed as 'offensive to public morals'. Daringly, El Shafee combines a heist thriller based around Cairo's subway with a portrait of his people, subtly conveying the message that they are so caught in the 'trap' of day-to-day survival that most cannot contemplate challenging President Mubarak's repression. While the story contains one mild sex scene and some edgy language in colloquial Egyptian instead of formal Arabic, what probably offended Mubarak far more was its thinly disguised critique of his regime and its advocacy of people power. Reflecting on the Arab Spring that followed, El Shafee told *Newsweek* on 25 June 2012 that his book had reached out to a 'growing community of readers crying out for freedom.' It had helped prepare them by showing how *Metro*'s hero 'discovers we're all locked up in jail but the door is wide open. That's what happened: people found these jailers were cowards; they wondered why they didn't make this revolution twenty years ago.' In post-Mubarak Egypt, however, despite appeals, there seems little chance of the ban on *Metro* being lifted soon, although it has helped to encourage the next wave of local cartoonists. In 2011, Mohammed Shennawy co-founded the street-level satirical magazine *Tok Tok*. 'Even if every artist in *Tok Tok* has his own point of view and his way of telling a story, we're all trying to document the current period in drawings, words and comics, a medium that was forgotten here for years.'[4]

Metro
Magdy El Shafee, 2008

Not only can the medium be forgotten, but so too can great swathes of the population, so-called 'minorities' – for example, women and people of different ages, abilities, races, classes and sexual orientations – who are less likely to see themselves and their experiences and views represented in what has been and remains in most countries a male-dominated medium. Or if they do, they can be portrayed in demeaning, even dehumanising ways. Comics have long relied on simplifying the complexities of real human beings down to caricatures, exaggerated, distorted and abstracted, to reveal their characteristics. Over the years, cartoonists pass down and add to an iconography, an armoury of symbols shared between artists and between readers. But there is a danger of these diverse, adaptable character types becoming standardised and generalised stereotypes and being used maliciously. In her strip commentary 'Stereotypical', lesbian cartoonist Kate Charlesworth uses her leather-jacketed mouthpiece Auntie Studs ('Do I look like your typical 39-year old dyke?') to explain what a cartoon stereotype is: 'It's an idea, trait or convention that's grown stale through fixed usage.' At their best, she sees them as 'shorthand for getting a load of information over in one shot … thus obviating the necessity for superfluous and extraneous verbiage', and insists that 'stereotypes are there for the subverting!' She demonstrates this in her witty final panel of 'the most insidious stereotype of all! The "Normal Family"!', shown as an advertiser's dream, all white, middle-class, heterosexual, beaming and outwardly respectable, by adding textual footnotes

disclosing their secrets. Defying their bland outward appearances, the pipe-smoking dad is revealed to be a wife-beater, the mother a rabid racist, their eldest daughter is having an affair and an IVF love-child with the woman next door, their sons are a trainee mugger and an auto-asphyxiator, and their youngest little girl is a playground bully! As Charlesworth advises, 'Remember, careless cartooning can cause offence.'[5]

Stereotypes are powerful and persistent. In the nineteenth and early twentieth century, American popular culture propagated 'humorous' racist stereotypes, including in comics, to make the injustices of slavery, segregation and imperialism seem almost rational and natural. Black people were caricatured not as individuals, but to conform to a standardised portrayal as minstrels and childlike simpletons, savages closer to monkeys than humans, their lips enlarged to fill the lower halves of their faces, dependent on and thankful to their white superiors. Black British graphic novelist Woodrow Phoenix sees this stereotype as 'the end result of a centuries-long campaign to make racism so unremarkable, so ordinary, that it is easy to perpetuate. The minstrel was and is a convenient shorthand for laziness, stupidity, greed, animality and otherness. Foreignness. The alien. The savage. The purpose of racist imagery is to deny reality … to flatten real people into unreal tokens, to remove their humanity so that it is easier to marginalise them and ultimately, to destroy them.' Though by no means the worst example, even the apparently sweet 'Pore Lil' Mose', one of

Pappa and The Black Hands
Anton Kannemeyer, 2009
Original artwork

Richard Outcault's follow-ups in 1900 to 'The Yellow Kid' before his 'Buster Brown' hit in 1902, and an early example of a black character starring in his own strip, built its comedy on the topsy-turvy absurdity of a smartly-dressed seven-year old black boy who lives on his own in New York with his animal friends and writes naively in rhyming couplets to his 'Dear Mammy' in Cottonville.

Over time, a few black cartoonists would be nationally syndicated in major American newspapers, starting in 1965 with Morrie Turner's 'Wee Pals'. His kids' comedy, a sort of ethnically diverse 'Peanuts', was initially bought by only five papers, but within three months of Martin Luther King Jr's assassination in 1968, over one hundred newspapers added the daily strip.

Earlier black cartoonists worked for the local black press, such as the *Chicago Defender*, founded in 1905 by Robert S. Abbott, which was the first to add a whole page of its own strips. When Leslie Rogers conceived a strip in 1920 about the ever-changing fortunes of one Bungleton Green, a new arrival to the city from the rural South, he did so without venom. Garrett Whyte dealt more pointedly with civil rights through a racist, crow-headed Southern politician, 'The Notorious Mr. Jim Crow' (below). In 1937, another black-owned paper, the weekly *Pittsburgh Courier*, introduced the country's first black woman cartoonist, Zelda Jackson 'Jackie' Ormes, and her feisty singer-dancer heroine Torchy Brown (left). Her name lives on in The Ormes Society, formed in October 2012 to support black female comics creators; it is heartening that it already counts almost fifty members.

Back in the late 1960s and early 1970s, despite being uncensored and taboo-smashing, the underground comix community based around San Francisco's counterculture was not all that racially concerned or diverse, with Manuel 'Spain' Rodriguez and Richard 'Grass' Green as its most prominent non-white participants. In fact, in the seminal *Zap Comix 1* in 1968, Robert Crumb would hark back to the minstrel tropes, usually with ironic, parodic and farcical intentions, while later he eulogised beloved blues and jazz musicians in biographical strips and bubble-gum card portraits. Europe has its own tradition of racist imagery and in the parallel Dutch underground of the early 1970s,

TORCHY Brown
by JACKIE ORMES
HEARTBEATS

TORCHY AND DAN HAVE MADE A HIT AT THE OPENING OF THEIR DANCE ENGAGEMENT AT THE SWANK SHORE CLUB. BUT TORCHY, IN LOVE WITH DAN, FINDS SUCCESS HAS BROUGHT DAN NEW INTERESTS.

SHE RETURNS TO THE CLUB LATE THAT NIGHT TO RETRIEVE SOME KEYS SHE'D LEFT IN THE DRESSING ROOM AND IS IN TIME TO SEE--

IT---IT'S DAN! AND THAT---THAT'S THE CHORUS GIRL HE WAS GETTING SO CHUMMY WITH BACKSTAGE!

HE--HE SAID HE COULDN'T GO OUT WITH ME TONIGHT. HE WAS TOO TIRED! I DIDN'T WANT TO BELIEVE HE WAS LYING--- I DIDN'T WANT TO!

HER MIND A JUMBLED, REELING THING, TORCHY MECHANICALLY RETRIEVED HER KEYS AND RETURNED TO THE NIGHT, HER HEART QUIVERING WITH THE ARROWS OF BETRAYAL---

I--(CHOKE)--I GUESS THERE'S NO USE FOOLING MYSELF ANY LONGER.

AIMLESSLY, NEITHER KNOWING NOR CARING WHERE, TORCHY WANDERED THROUGH THE NIGHT, DRAWING THE DARK AROUND HER LIKE A PROTECTIVE CLOAK, GRATEFUL FOR THE SHADOWS THAT HID THE TEARS UPON HER FACE--

HE SAID HE LOVED ME--THAT NOTHING WOULD EVER CHANGE. I--I GUESS THE LAUGH'S ON ME--ONLY HOW CAN YOU LAUGH WHEN YOUR HEART IS CRYING!

MAYBE IT'S FUNNY OF ME, BUT I DON'T HATE DAN BECAUSE OF--(CHOKE)--WHAT'S HAPPENED. I DO LOVE HIM TOO MUCH FOR THAT. I JUST SEEM SORT OF, WELL----DEAD, INSIDE! IT'S AS IF THE WORLD SUDDENLY STOPPED.

THE HOURS STOLE AWAY, UNNOTICED BY TORCHY, TILL FINALLY, DAWN LIFTED THE CURTAIN OF NIGHT----A NIGHT OF TEARS AND BROKEN HOPES, VANISHED DREAMS AND REMEMBERED YEARNINGS----

IT---IT'S MORNING! I--I'VE BEEN HERE HOURS AND IT'S SEEMED LIKE MINUTES! I'VE GOT TO GO HOME AND GET A LITTLE REST OR I WON'T BE ABLE TO GO ON TONIGHT!

Copyright 1950, The Smith-Mann Syndicate.

BUT, OUT OF THE NIGHT OF BITTER TEARS AND TORN DREAMS, A NEW RESOLVE COMES, A NEW KIND OF HOPE THAT, RIGHT OR WRONG, STEMMED FROM A LOVE TOO GREAT TO GIVE UP---

I'M NOT GOING TO SAY ANYTHING ABOUT WHAT I SAW TONIGHT. MAYBE THIS IS JUST A PASSING PHASE IN DAN'S HEART ---ONLY AN INTERMEZZO NOT WORTH BOTHERING ABOUT.

ANYWAY, I'LL BE NEAR HIM, DANCING WITH HIM EVERY NIGHT, SEEING HIS SMILE, HEARING HIS LAUGH. AND, ONE OF THESE DAYS, I'LL MAKE HIM MY OWN AGAIN--- MY VERY OWN.

BUT CAN TORCHY RECAPTURE THE LOVE THAT ONCE WAS HERS? OR WILL SHE FIND SHE CHASES A RAINBOW THAT NEVER REALLY EXISTED?

FOLLOW TORCHY NEXT WEEK AND EVERY WEEK IN HER STORY, THE STORY OF ONE HEART'S SEARCH FOR HAPPINESS!

Joost Swarte also drew from these tropes and Hergé's portrayals of black characters, not least in his Jopo de Pojo character, analysed by Chris Ware as a 'disquieting amalgam of animated cartoon African-American stereotype and lily-white Euro-Tintin.' Is a lack of any racist intention enough to allay concerns about comics artists making such retro-chic revivals today? In the opinion of Woodrow Phoenix, 'continuing to use this symbol now is the worst kind of thoughtlessness.'

And what about the effects of Swarte's sources in *Tintin in the Congo*? The recent widespread availability in bookstores of Hergé's patronising depictions of Africans in this second adventure, originally serialised in 1930–1, have stirred complaints. It was the 1946 colour version of the book, so controversial that it was translated into English only in 2005 and remains unpublished in the USA, which sparked calls in 2007 from the British Commission for Racial Equality for the book to be banned. Circumspect publishers Egmont had placed a warning of racist content on a protective band around their edition and added an introduction explaining the historical context. Finally, British retail chains refused to remove the book altogether but restricted its sale to the adult graphic novel section or to people aged sixteen and over.

In Belgium, Hergé's homeland and the colonial power guilty of the genocide of some eleven million people in the Belgian Congo, Bienvenu Mbutu Mondondo, a Congolese immigrant and political science student, and the Belgian Council of Black Associations, pursued their case to ban the book as far as the Brussels Appellate Court. They lost, in part because of their mistaken understanding of what legally constitutes harrassment, as Belgian post-doctoral researcher Jogchum Vrielink explains. Under Belgium's Anti-Racism Act, 'the prohibition of harrassment requires the violation of the dignity of one or more concrete persons, and not of an abstract group such as "the Congolese" or black people in general … clearly, this language was not intended to cover mediated and impersonal types of "group defamation" by means of the mass-media or comic books.' The applicants' other claims based on hate speech provisions in the Act also failed owing to what the Court judged as 'evident absence of the required malicious intent', whether of Hergé, who died in 1983, or of the present publishers and copyright holders.[6] The plaintiffs' lawyer Ahmed L'Hedim had stated, 'This comic should be contextualised, relativised, at least, because it conveys negative images',[7] but the Court ruled that to require a warning to be added to the book would interfere both with freedom of expression and the work's integrity. So it remains to be seen if any such contextualising concessions may be made to future editions in Belgium, along the lines of the British version. Even as intelligent and well-travelled a comics creator as manga master Osamu Tezuka could fall back on racist stereotypes as late as 1968, when depicting South Pacific islanders in *Swallowing the Earth*. At least Kodansha

FOR YOU TO BE ABLE TO CONTRIBUTE EFFICACIOUSLY IN A UTILITARIAN MODUS.

SO, IF YOU ARE A GUBERNATORIAL CANDIDATE

AND YOU DON'T GO THROUGH THE RITUAL

OF EVEN READING NEWSPAPERS

YOU DON'T BATHE YOURSELF IN THE AQUA OF THE POLITICAL CROSS CURRENTS,

THEN YOU ARE GOING TO BE DEUCED;

Captain Rugged
Keziah Jones (writer) and Native Maqari (artist),
2013

bowed to complaints when reprinting this tale and added a disclaimer. In the case of Hergé, while it is little excuse that he was reflecting the commonly held prejudices of his times and of his editor, Catholic priest Abbé Wallez, the continued availability of *Tintin in the Congo* means it can now be re-evaluated, not least by the Congolese themselves, as evidence of how ignorant the colonialists were towards Africans.

In this process, Tintin is also a stereotype ripe for subversion. Anton Kannemeyer, a white cartoonist-provocateur in South Africa, has been fierce and fearless in skewering the Apartheid system and the broader legacy of colonialism since co-founding the underground

anthology *Bitterkomix* in 1992. In the deeply discomforting 'Pappa and The Black Hands' (p.75), Kannemeyer reinterprets a famous environmentally incorrect 'comedy' hunting scene from Hergé's *Tintin in the Congo* by ageing the boy-reporter into a balding father figure, close to Kannemeyer's own appearance, and blacking up Snowy the dog into 'Blackie'. Whereas Tintin in the original keeps shooting at what he thinks is one seemingly indestructible antelope, only to find that he has killed a whole herd, Kannemeyer's Pappa does the same, but slays not one but nine black Africans, a comment on the idea that to him they all look identical. Pappa then strolls off with a sackful of their severed hands, a reference to Belgium's brutal punishment of rubber-plantation workers who failed to meet their quotas. Kannemeyer explained to Xavier Guilbert, 'I wanted to create an archetype, or a stereotypical kind of colonialist. To try and create a counter figure – what is the ultimate white, as opposed to the ultimate black, kind of character. A lot of my work deals with race, so I had those two poles that I had to create. The other thing of course is that I, myself, live in Africa, and obviously all those issues of guilt and what happened before, I'm always aware of it. I'm working with it all the time.'[8] Now a father himself, Kannemeyer is conscious of how 'this iconography kind of sticks. Even if you're not a racist, it can become an undercurrent that will maintain that there's some kind of superiority.'

Fortunately, there are alternative ideas and imagery in today's comics to counter this undercurrent. In

Deogratias: A Tale of Rwanda (2000), Belgian artist J.P. Stassen conveys the nightmare of the country's genocide in 1994, never directly, but obliquely. He intercuts between scenes before and after the massacres, contrasting sunnier frameless flashbacks with the harrowing after-effects on one young man called Deogratias (or 'Thanks be to God', an ironic name in the circumstances). In a nod to the colonialist classroom scene in *Tintin in the Congo*, Stassen shows Deogratias as a boy being taught about the country's different 'races', Hutu and Tutsi. Once out of school, Deogratias, a Hutu, tells his female Tutsi school friends, 'The teacher is a fool'. Tragically, this ethnic division was worsened under white Belgian rule, which privileged the taller, more fair-skinned Tutsi with education in Catholic schools and jobs over the Hutu, stoking the inter-tribal tensions behind the genocide higher. Forced to choose sides, Deogratias witnesses and participates in horrors that shatter his hold on sanity, driving him to drink, delusions that he has become a dog, and poisonous revenge. By individualising such a massive tragedy, Stassen fosters a personal connection and empathy in the reader. He also subtly indicts the political influence of the Catholic hierarchy. When his book won France's Ecumenical Comics Award for 2000, he refused to accept it because of the Church's role in Rwanda. Stassen is now married and lives there with his family.

Guadaloupe was the home of Aristophane Boulon, who moved to Paris at the age of eight. In his three deftly characterised tales of *The Zabime*

The Zabime Sisters
Aristophane Boulon ('Aristophane'), 1996

Sisters, Aristophane (his comics penname) evokes the overheated days and emotions of three girls coming of age on the Caribbean island (right). In lushly sensual chiaroscuro, his almost Fauvist brushwork in black ink captures the out-of-focus heat-haze and the vivid patterning and blurring boundaries between the children's bodies, sweating and glowing, the fabrics of their clothes and the vegetation all around them. Aristophane once said that in his mind he always had 'a phrase our teacher told us. "In painting, everything has been explored. The future belongs to comics."' Aristophane died much too young, aged only 37 in 2004, but his extraordinary oeuvre proves that his teacher was right.

Another more urban portrait of adolescence was written by Marguerite Abouet, who grew up in the Ivory Coast until 1983 when, aged twelve, she relocated to a Paris suburb. Abouet wanted to recollect her upbringing during a prosperous postcolonial period in her homeland's history. Vividly illustrated by her French husband Clément Oubrerie, their six-volume series deals with the everyday dramas of the maturing Aya and her friends and family caught between new freedoms and old traditions (pp.84–5). Abouet reveals an unfamiliar Africa, rarely shown in other Western media, as she told *Wild River Review*: 'The easygoing and careless impression of Africa found in *Aya* fortunately still exists, even today. African women finally share the same dreams of other women on the planet, and I wish only to show their daily lives filled with hopes and desires to perform as modern

Quando nacqui, nel 1926, villaggio di Madgalinavsky, regione di Dnepropetrovsk, mio padre partì e si fece un'altra famiglia.

Mia madre faceva un mestiere da uomini, dissodava la terra, con la zappa.

Ma voleva che io studiassi, e mise da parte dei soldi per questo.

Mi piaceva. E non solo per lei, che mi insegnava qualunque cosa.

Cucinare, cucire, ogni faccenda domestica. Perfino a costruire un pollaio.

ABOVE:
American Born Chinese
Gene Yang, 2006

RIGHT:
Ukrainian Notebooks
Igor Tuveri ('Igort'), 2010

OVERLEAF:
Aya: Love in Yop City
Marguerite Abouet & Clément Oubrerie, 2008

women in Africa.'[9] In another portrait of Africa, Keziah Jones and Native Maqari only slightly distort the issues of contemporary political corruption in Lagos, Nigeria, exposed by their unlikely crusader *Captain Rugged* (p.79).

Other negative stereotypes have been addressed directly by graphic novelists keenly aware of these images' insidious, viral power. In 2003, the late Will Eisner challenged the hook-nosed, hunch-backed caricature of the Sephardic Jew, which originated in the 1780s as an accurate enough observation of an East London social type, but was distorted into a damning caricature, popularised through cartoons such as George Cruikshank's illustrations of Fagin in Charles Dickens's *Oliver Twist*, and the anti-semitic iconography in Nazi propaganda. In *Fagin the Jew*, Eisner re-cast the rogue based on historical evidence that Fagin was more likely to have been a poor Ashkenazi from Central Europe, and gave him a very different appearance, background and character. Audaciously, in the partly autobiographical *American Born Chinese* in 2006, Gene Yang adapts the offensive buck-toothed Chinese stereotype to positive use as Cousin Chin-Kee, a satire of the worst racist prejudice, whose beheading symbolises a bullied Asian-American schoolboy's eventual self-acceptance and self-confidence (above). Yang is alert to the risk of perpetuating such imagery, sometimes still dredged up by insensitive political cartoonists, but reflects, 'I think it's a danger I can live with. In order for us to defeat our enemy, he must first be made visible.'

Also in need of being 'made visible' are still more varied, individual, revelatory portraits which reaffirm our shared humanity. Luckily, the diversity of practitioners and protagonists in comics has never been richer. The lives and loves of Hispanic-American lesbian 'locas' and Latina matriarchs fill Jaime and Gilbert Hernandez's ongoing *Love and Rockets* sagas. The ways of early twentieth-century Quebecois countryfolk are brought to life in the affectionate serial *Magasin Général* by Régis Loisel and Jean-Louis Tripp. Asian-Americans' struggles are evoked in *Shortcomings* by Adrian Tomine, who tackles the strained relations between Japanese and Korean Americans, and in *Skim* by Mariko and Jillian Tamaki, narrated as the diary of a half-Japanese goth loner who falls in love with her favourite female teacher.

For his remarkable graphic reportage *Ukrainian Notebooks* (right),the Italian artist Igort spent months in the former Soviet country unearthing memories of the Holodomor, 'The Hunger', a devastating man-made famine engineered in 1932–3 by Stalin to enforce his farming collectivisation programme and shatter the peasantry's independent spirit. For decades it was a state secret. Its repercussions and further injustices have not ceased to this day. Interviewing survivors, Igort found that 'These people have no voice, nobody had listened. They were not used to speaking. Why don't we know about these things? So many of us are bored by the nothing that is always told in comics, the emptiness. I think these are the new ways of storytelling.'

NO ONE ASKED YOU TO TAKE ON THE JOB OF BEING MY FATHER'S MISTRESS.

SORRY TO SAY IT, AYA, BUT YOUR FATHER WAS AFTER ME FOR MONTHS.

HE KEPT COMING AROUND LIKE A BEE TAKES TO HONEY...

HE TOLD ME HIS WIFE WAS INFERTILE, THAT HE HAD NO KIDS...

HE SAID HE WANTED TO LEAVE HER, BUT THAT SHE WAS SO SICK HE HAD TO DO IT GENTLY.

THAT'S NOT TRUE! YOU'RE LYING!

BY THE TIME I FOUND HIM OUT, IT WAS TOO LATE: RAY AND PAMELA WERE ALREADY THERE.

RAY AND PAMELA?

YOUR BROTHER AND SISTER, AYA.

AS LONG AS IGNACE DID HIS PART, I WAS WILLING TO KEEP A LOW PROFILE. BUT DUMPING THE THREE OF US IN A ONE-ROOM APARTMENT? NO WAY!!

TAXI!

WHAT YOU'RE DOING IS CRUEL!

Y'KNOW, AYA, LIFE IS CRUEL SOMETIMES. YOU'VE JUST GOT TO MAKE THE BEST OF IT, DÊH!

FIRST-PERSONS SINGULAR:
AUTOBIOGRAPHY IN COMICS

6

After the blossoming in France of *bandes dessinées* for adults following the protests of May 1968 and their accompanying cultural shifts, French comics had reached something of a regressive low-point by 1985. Women were poorly represented in the male-dominated medium, as characters and as creators. Odile in Chantal Montellier's *Odile et les crocodiles* (right) was the rare exception of a complex female lead, a rape victim denied justice and driven to revenge. Fuelled by Montellier's political views, Odile was hailed by one reviewer as the agent most likely to end the crocodiles' reign; from today's perspective, Montellier reflects, 'Alas, they have thick skins. But Odile and the game are not over yet.'

In 1985, Montellier became one of four French women cartoonists who decided they had seen enough of the way most of the country's male comics industry was heading. With Florence Cestac, Nicole Claveloux and Jeanne Puchol, she spoke out for change in a manifesto published in the leading newspaper *Le Monde* on 27 January, coinciding with the 12th Angoulême International Comics Festival: 'It's distressing that this so-called new medium is crippled by the oldest and dirtiest macho fantasies. Distressing to see most comic magazines follow suit and take the easiest path ... Retro, fine racial humour, society gossip, colonial nostalgia, gratuitous violence ... fetishism, sexism and infantilism are the order of the day ... Because we love certain comics, because we want magazines to be at the service of creators and not just sellers, because

every day they are reducing the space afforded to creativity in favour of uniformity, we wanted to respond by hoping that this letter finds an echo among authors as well as readers.'

Others signed this manifesto, and its echoes would reverberate eventually across the landscape of comics, not only in France. Change is possible, in comics as in society, but there is always resistance re-imposing the status quo. More often, radical, lasting change comes from creators, publishers and promoters who are mavericks, outsiders, less encumbered by the need to make quick profits and satisfy shareholders. In France, a wave of publishers sprang up such as L'Association in 1990, a collective run by creators, and Ego Comme X in 1994, specialising in autobiography. As an alternative to the limiting Francophone industrial standard of the large, forty-eight-page, full-colour hardback album like *Asterix*, these independents let creators work to whatever length their story required and often in more compact formats closer to literary prose. The French edition of Art Spiegelman's *Maus* in 1987, and the boom in translated manga soon after, helped the black-and-white paperback to catch on and become part of '*La nouvelle bande dessinée*'. The number of original graphic novels published each year in France has almost quadrupled from 1,137 in 2000 to 4,109 in 2012, of which 12 per cent were by women, still a minority but on the rise, a very different picture to that of 1985.

Maus has had an undeniable impact on the international graphic novel

Odile et les crocodiles
Chantal Montellier, 1984

ENFIN! COMME DIT LE POÈTE, POUR L'AMOUR ON NE DEMANDE PAS AUX FEMMES D'AVOIR INVENTÉ LA POUDRE.

ET JOLIE COMME VOUS L'ÊTES ON NE PEUT QU'ÊTRE DISPOSÉ À VOUS AIMER...

N'EST-CE PAS!?

GLLP!

J'AI D'ABORD PENSÉ À ME LIVRER À LA POLICE...

13

movement and especially on the growth in autobiographical comics. Who would have thought that the most painful family history during and since the Holocaust could be told afresh in comics and engage with readers who might not choose to read a text novel or watch a movie on such a difficult subject? *Maus* is an example of what American cartoonist Lynda Barry calls 'story power', which 'seems to come from a need to understand that thing we can't think out loud. It comes in the form of an experience, even one we don't want in real life.'[1] Autobiographical comics have that story power to admit us into the sometimes problematic or distressing lives of others, people we may otherwise never know, and to find perspectives on our own. Spiegelman fully understands the complications of using animal stereotypes when he portrays Jews as vulnerable mice victims and Germans as cruel cat predators, a discomforting metaphor on multiple levels, because the Nazis likened Jews to rats and used rat poison to exterminate them. *Maus* is also an astutely self-aware work, a blend of biography and autobiography. It is as much about Art Spiegelman's own conflicts: he is

the child of survivors who uses the recording of his father's memories to make a book that helps him to connect and somehow communicate with his parent, yet he is also plagued with guilt about the book's success being based on his parents' ordeals.

Before *Maus*, two remarkable earlier examples of graphic memoir were ahead of their time. Olaf Gulbranson was a Norwegian-born cartoonist who drew for the German satirical magazine *Simplicissimus*. In 1934, entering his sixties as professor at the Munich Arts Academy, he composed a lyrical journey through his past in *Es War Einmal* ('Once Upon A Time'). Drawn and written in the same pen and hand, his recollections in neat capitals wrap themselves around his precise, economic illustrations. In 1936, the German-Jewish student Charlotte Salomon secured a place at the Berlin Academy of Fine Art. To escape Hitler's persecution, her family moved to Nice in the south of France, where in late 1941, aged twenty-four, she began painting *Leben? oder Theater?* ('Life? or Theatre?') (above), aware that her time was limited. This outpouring of 769 gouache paintings charts her life so far,

from childhood holidays to rejection by an art tutor, and her family's tragedies such as the suicides of her mother and grandmother. Initially, she composed her texts on separate overlays, but later added dialogue onto her increasingly expressive artworks, all with suggested musical accompaniment. Fearing that the Nazis would find her, Salomon entrusted this narrative suite to a friend, saying, 'Keep this safe, it is my whole life.' She was gassed in Auschwitz in 1943. Her work survived and since the 1960s has been more widely exhibited and published. Compared by critics to opera, theatre and film, *Leben? oder Theater?* comes closest to being an utterly modern graphic novel.

Such raw candour was forbidden in commercial, family-friendly comics. Artists might sometimes playfully portray themselves but usually at a remove, perhaps making an introduction or aside, or interacting with their fictional characters. Two unusual exceptions were both ex-soldiers' accounts of the Second World War. Entirely out of place amidst the otherwise mild kiddies' fare in *Adventure Comic Annual*, an undated British gift book from the mid-1950s, was the short story 'I Was A Jap Slave' (left), the crude but heartfelt record of presumably the uncredited author's imprisonment and escape. In various DC war comics between 1970 and 1977, Sam Glanzman related nearly fifty four-page vignettes about himself and his fellow sailors serving in the Navy aboard the 'USS Stevens', later expanding his own tale into the two-part graphic novel *A Sailor's Story*.

The notion of comics as a viable medium to disclose challenging and life-changing private matters and express real psychological anguish was first decisively proved in 1972 in Japan and in the USA. Early one August morning in 1945, six-year old Keiji Nakazawa was on his way to school in Hiroshima when the American atomic bomb 'Little Boy' was dropped, annihilating over 100,000 people and devastating the lives of thousands more. Of his family, only young Keiji, his mother and one brother survived and endured the dreadful aftermath. Nakazawa's mother made great sacrifices to help him fulfil his dream of becoming a manga author, but she died prematurely of leukemia in 1966, her cremated bones crumbling to white powder. The bomb's radiation had claimed another victim. Haunted by his mother's death and by the horrors he had lived through, Nakazawa vowed to 'do battle through manga'. Soon after the funeral, he vented his grief and anger in an unbridled revenge

fantasy, *Pelted by Black Rain*, about an A-bomb survivor using black-market weapons to assassinate Americans. Rejected as too provocative and anti-American, it was eventually published by the minor publisher of the adult *Manga Punch* as the first of eight bleak *Black* tales highlighting the terrible consequences of the war.

Nakazawa had more luck regularly crafting less strident anti-war stories in, of all places, a highly commercial comic for boys, *Weekly Shonen Jump*. Out of these came the invitation in 1972 to draw the opening forty-eight-page story in a special edition of *Jump* in which various creators recounted true tales from their lives, a landmark in itself. Nakazawa's entry was 'I Saw It', a moving forty-eight-page autobiography. This prompted the editor to commission a long weekly serial based on his life, and in June 1973 'Barefoot Gen' began (above). Although Nakazawa changed certain events to make them more dramatic, it stands as an only slightly fictionalised chronicle of his real experiences before and after the Bomb. While critical of America, he attacks Japan's wartime militarist regime and puts the ultimate blame for the atomic bombings on Emperor Hirohito, a contentious view in Japan. The series eventually reached ten volumes and more than 2,500 pages, but not without struggle. After eighteen months, his editor left *Jump* and the very mainstream weekly dropped Nakazawa, who had to pursue serialisation in more marginal, left-leaning magazines. Still, awareness spread through the international peace movement, and

ABOVE: **Barefoot Gen: The Day After**
Keiji Nakazawa, 1973

RIGHT:
Binky Brown Meets The Holy Virgin Mary
Justin Green, 1972
Original artwork

in 1976 activists set up Project Gen in America to translate the series. One of the first books of manga ever put into English, *Barefoot Gen* is outspoken, often bluntly horrifying, its traditional boys' manga exaggerations jarring to Western eyes, but ultimately inspirational, bringing human scale and courage to almost unfathomable suffering.

Among other manga authors using forms of autobiography are Shigeru Mizuki who also condemned Japan's military in *Onwards Towards Our Noble Deaths* in 1973, his version of a disastrous wartime mission in New Guinea, and Yoshihiru Tatsumi who recreates, in *A Drifting Life* (2008), his adolescent fervour for making comics during the volatile post-war period. Since the late 1980s, Japanese men's general interest magazines have become the surprising outlet for autobiographical gag strips by women in a simplified comedy style, so-called 'essay manga', ranging from Shungiku Uchida's 'We Are Reproducing', about childbirth and childcare, to Tenten Hosokawa's 'My Partner Became Depressed', about her out-of-work husband's depression.

Meanwhile, back in 1972, across the Pacific in San Francisco, the scars of another damaged childhood drove Justin Green to express himself through the new uncensored form of underground comics. To assuage his extreme sexual guilt indoctrinated in him by strict Catholic nuns, Green shows how, as a pubescent boy, he constructed elaborate rituals such as hitting his head on his bed's

headboard to drive out 'impure thoughts', behaviour that today would be diagnosed and treated as obsessive-compulsive disorder (p.91). Imagining multiple penises replacing his fingers, feet and everyday objects while sitting in his underpants, circled by figures of the Madonna, Green would agonise about his 'pecker rays' aligning with and desecrating any nearby church. The sheer intensity of labour and frankness needed over seven months to produce the almost illuminated *Binky Brown Meets The Holy Virgin Mary* – a rare example of a full-length, forty-four-page solo underground comic – make its creation like yet another penance, if not an exorcism. As Green stated, 'It was done out of internal necessity.' Underground comics had set out to break taboos, to shock and outrage, but Green helped bring a more meaningful agenda, transforming his panels into confession boxes, where nothing needed to be hidden or denied anymore. His example quickly galvanised his peers, including Robert Crumb, Aline Kominsky (Crumb's girlfriend and eventual wife), Art Spiegelman, and successive generations in America and beyond into exposing their most personal issues. As the British art critic Waldemar Januszczak wrote, 'When the neurotics appropriated the strip cartoon, we witnessed the ideal marriage of form and content. They subverted its innocence and filled its thought balloons with their wretched, guilt-sodden soliloquies. The strip cartoon turned out to be a splendid medium for confessions. And we, the audience, found ourselves called upon to perform the duties of the Catholic priest.'[2]

Émile
Fabrice Neaud, 2000

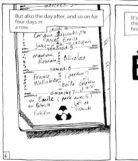

Forgiveness, or at least self-forgiveness, do not necessarily follow from unbottling your feelings onto the page in words and pictures. At least now, Green says he can cope with his disorder and resist any 'residual reflexes' by avoiding dope and drink.[3] Autobiographical comics can carry consequences, however. Cartoonists have been criticised, sometimes ostracised, by the living people they present in their comics. Craig Thompson was raised by fundamentalist Christian parents who did not take kindly to his memoir *Blankets* making public their repressive upbringing and his fraught efforts to rebel and find freedom and romance. David B. weathered similar complaints from his mother as he serialised his six-volume record of his elder brother's epilepsy and the family's desperate search for a cure, and incorporated her misgivings within the pages of *Epileptic* itself.

Also from France, Fabrice Neaud faced issues following the third volume in his diaristic series *Journal* in 1999, in which he chronicled his deep, unrequited love over eighteen months for a male friend, whom he drew realistically and recognisably but re-named as 'Dominique' in the book. Its publication by Ego Comme X in Angoulême complicated Neaud's personal life there, now that it was out in the open. To avoid further homophobic repercussions, in his next graphic novella Neaud removed his lover 'Émile', and in fact all human beings except in drawn photographs, showing only objects and settings (p.93). He removed himself entirely, illustrating and narrating everything

from his subjective viewpoint. These absurd absences only emphasise the social exclusion, invisibility and risks involved in participating in homosexual relationships in a regional French city. Neaud's self-censorship ended up with him all but abandoning further autobiographical comics, after another lover succeeded in getting an injunction forbidding Neaud from depicting him. As for Dominique's attitude, Neaud explained, 'If [he] wanted to sue me, he would win the case and the book would be withdrawn from the trade. But Dominique, who told me that he thought I could have been harder on him, and who is an artist himself, also said, "I appreciate the book as a work of art, so being an artist I can't tell you that you don't have the right to do it." But not everyone is that smart.'[4]

Neaud draws from models and photographs, lending his comics at times an almost documentary credibility. Others, such as Luis Garciá from Spain and Boston's Karl Stevens, have done likewise. A good deal of the now considerable autobiographical genre worldwide tends towards the other end of the spectrum based on unpolished, quite child-like drawing styles, suggesting urgency and immediacy. Frequently, the only way to start getting such atypical approaches published is for the artists to do so themselves, as in the cases of Sylvie Rancourt's rudimentary but entirely effective self-portrayals as a Montreal lap-dancer in *Melody*, or Nicola Streeten's seemingly spontaneous but considered and heartfelt self-expression on the effects of losing her two-year-old son in *Billy, Me and You*. Such creators' idiosyncratic techniques and lack of slickness, whether by conscious choice or naturally, seem to emphasise their work's individuality and integrity. Style can say a lot. Art Spiegelman initially experimented with a heavily rendered, scraper-board approach on *Maus*, which he had applied in 1972 to his first autobiographical story, 'Prisoner on the Hell Planet', but it proved too angst-ridden and sympathy-seeking. His actual style for *Maus* is deliberately modest and clear as a diagram, drawn unusually at the same size as the printed page, giving the reader the impression that they have found the original surviving manuscript.

Two American women were at the vanguard of writing their lives with fresh directness, Aline Kominsky and Lynda Barry. In the 1970s, Kominsky brought an unmediated rawness to her unflattering self-portrayals, starting in *Wimmen's Comix* (1972). Barely influenced at all by comics, she tapped into her art school training and drew from Outsider Art and Art Brut. After falling out with the *Wimmen's Comix* collective, she and Diane Noomin quit to set up their own edgier anthology *Twisted Sisters*, whose first cover featured Kominsky sitting on the toilet, grunting and worrying about the calories in a cheese enchilada. With Robert Crumb, she would go on to create their unique *Dirty Laundry* comics about their life together, the two of them drawing themselves in the same panel.

The shock of Crumb's unfettered sexual revelations motivated Lynda Barry:

'What Crumb gave to me was the feeling that you could draw anything.'[5] Encouragement also came from her art tutor Marilyn Frasca at the non-traditional Evergreen State College in Olympia, Washington, whose cross-disciplinary workshop course, *The Intensive Journal*, combined painting and drawing with writing and reading. Frasca noticed her student's progress: 'In her writing she learned to follow leads given by one drawing to the next and proceeded with courage and good humour to develop a stunning body of work.' A Filipino-Irish-Norwegian 'odd duck', Barry has used her teacher's process since the 1980s in what she calls her 'autobifictionalography' about girlhood, instinctively fusing actual and imagined memories (pp.96–7).

Looking back through the eyes of your childhood self can provide a clarifying lens onto the past. Marjane Satrapi, Zeina Abirached and Marzena Sawa recreate their growing up – in Islamic Iran, in war-torn Beirut, and in Communist Poland – and bring out their youthful confusions, insights and lessons from these revolutionary times. Compelling family histories do not always have to draw on such momentous world events; so-called 'normal' life can be momentous too. Comics may serve as a medium of memorialisation, reconnection and sometimes reconciliation, notably by children towards their parents, a recurrent theme. Raymond Briggs paid a tender tribute to his parents in *Ethel & Ernest* after their deaths, acknowledging the enormous changes they had coped with throughout their lives. Before it

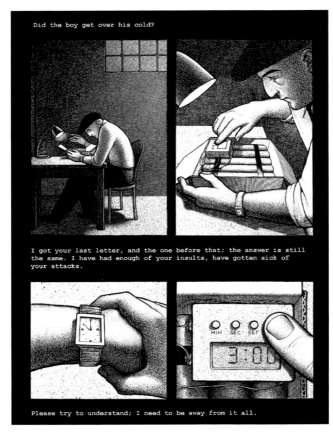

Did the boy get over his cold?

I got your last letter, and the one before that; the answer is still the same. I have had enough of your insults, have gotten sick of your attacks.

Please try to understand; I need to be away from it all.

becomes too late, Aapo Rapi in Finland has transcribed in *Meti* his widowed grandmother's oral history into comics, helping him to understand what she has gone through and what makes her who she is. Providing valuable accounts for anyone faced with ageing, ailing relatives, Joyce Farmer in *Special Exits*, Sarah Leavitt in *Tangles* and Brian Fies in *Mom's Cancer* share the demands and rewards of living with illness through their parents' twilight years.

Other cartoonists have needed more distance and hindsight to deal with unresolved grievances. In *Fun Home*, lesbian cartoonist Alison Bechdel rediscovers her links to her late father, a closeted gay teacher, through their shared love of literature and their secret homosexuality, although her feelings about her mother, still very much alive, are harder for her to disentangle in the sequel *Are You My Mother?* David Small's unloving parents caused him considerable psychological and physical harm – his mother was cold and easily angered, his father was a radiologist whose overdosing of X-rays on a cyst on

David's neck gave him a throat cancer which cost him his voice. Drawing became the boy's escape. Forty years on, drawing *Stitches* is a testament to his survival and his acceptance of his parents and himself. Nina Bunjevac lost her father, a Serbian nationalist exiled to Canada, where he died in an explosion linked to an attempted terrorist plot in August 1977. It was only in 2009 that Bunjavac could confront this through her story *August 1977* (above). Her richly pointillist, shadow-filled panels counterpoint the typed narration extracted from a real letter to her father written by her mother, and from an imaginary letter to him by the adult Nina. 'I created *August 1977* as a symbolic recreation of the last three hours of my father's life and as an attempt to reject his ideology, and patriarchy itself.'

Joe Sacco has made some self-deprecating autobiographical comics, but he is best known for his cartoon reportage in which he puts himself second to the people he interviews in warzones such as Palestine and Bosnia. Unapologetically subjective, Sacco shows the journalistic process, the exposure to risk, as he seeks out the victims and witnesses, the players and fixers, and uncovers the kinds of unreported stories lost and ignored in our news-saturated culture. This is what Sacco calls 'slow journalism'. Filing his comics like a reporter, he signs each page off with the date he completes them. He never depicts his eyes through his round glasses. His expressionless and enigmatic look conceals his own feelings and focuses on the more important feelings of others.

ABOVE:
'August 1977' from Heartless
Nina Bunjevac, 2010

RIGHT:
The Photographer
Didier Lefèvre, Emmanuel Guilbert and Frédéric Lemercier, 2004

OTHER WOUNDED PEOPLE HAVE BEEN LAID DOWN IN A LARGE, DARK ROOM WITH ONE SKYLIGHT. IT'S THE VILLAGE BAKERY. IT'S FULL OF PEOPLE AND WHISPERS. JOHN, JULIETTE, AND I MAKE OUR WAY THROUGH.

SEVERAL WOMEN ARE THERE, SOME OF THEM WITH THEIR FACES UNCOVERED.

ASK THEM IF I CAN TAKE PICTURES.

I'M ALLOWED TO DO SO.

IN A CORNER, A WOMAN WITH A WHITE HEADSCARF IS WATCHING OVER TWO OF HER CHILDREN, A TEENAGE GIRL AND A BABY, BOTH BLOODIED. THE LITTLE BOY IS MAYBE TWO OR THREE. HE HARDLY MOVES BUT FROM TIME TO TIME LETS OUT A LITTLE WAIL OF "AOH."

"AOH."

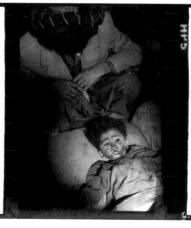

"AOH."

By doing this, Sacco believes his readers will find it easier to put themselves into his shoes and experience the events themselves. In his comic-strip travelogues, Quebecois animator Guy Delisle is less investigative reporter than visitor, as bemused, sometimes as baffled, as the reader, but ferreting out subtle revelations during his or his wife's peripatetic assignments, so far to Shenzen in China, Pyongyang in North Korea, Burma, and Jerusalem.

Emmanuel Guibert omits himself completely from his graphic novels, but they are based on the profound friendships he forms and on the anecdotes and documentation he gathers from them. His comics are biographies, but Guibert's presence is always felt on the page, the silent other half of the conversation, the listener, observer and translator of their lives. French photo-journalist Didier Lefèvre showed Guibert box after box of unpublished photographs from his gruelling mission in 1986 with Doctors Without Borders to bring medical care to both sides of the Afghanistan conflict. In the three volumes of *The Photographer* (2003, 2004 and 2006), Guibert and graphic designer-colourist Frédéric Lemercier re-tell Lefèvre's tale using his photographic contact sheets like comics panels and filling in the gaps, those scenes and conversations not caught on camera, with drawings and text (p.99). Guibert first met the American Alan Cope when the former GI was sixty-nine. Though separated by almost forty years, the two men bonded and Guibert taped hours of Cope's anecdotes, which the cartoonist started

to illustrate. The graphic novels *Alan's War* and its sequel, *Alan's Childhood*, have preserved and prolonged their friendship and enable us, too, to befriend this endearing raconteur.

Creators attuned to the fleeting, earthy poetry of the everyday can distill their observations into comics. The late Harvey Pekar pointed the way in *American Splendor*, defiantly self-published since 1976 'from the streets of Cleveland' and illustrated by his friend and fellow record-collector Robert Crumb and many other cartoonists. Eschewing the expectations of punchlines or twist endings, of conventional story structure, Pekar celebrated the un-splendid, the extraordinary in the ordinary that so often slips by. A Pandora's box of subject matter was suddenly opened up for comics. Not long after, Edmond Baudoin in France and Eddie Campbell in Britain began their explorations. Baudoin's dancing brushwork and Campbell's Letratone Impressionism enhance their observational writing. In *Alec: Love and Beerglasses* (1985), Campbell's alter ego muses, 'I had no ambition beyond life's daily round and the weekend celebration of it.' Around this time in Canada's alternative comics, the 'Toronto Three', Seth, Chester Brown and Joe Matt, stand out, including each other in some of their autobiographical work. Brown and Matt have been especially forthright, telling more than you might want to know about paying for prostitutes or fixating on porn videos. The French-Canadian Julie Doucet also held little back in her feverish

Je suis au festival de L. Installée à une table, je dédicace les livres devant une file d'acheteurs. J'exécute de petits autoportraits pour chacun d'eux. Je me rends compte que je m'en sors mal. Les portraits ne sont pas ressemblants. Je les rate les uns après les autres. Je m'en rends compte et je n'ose pas lever les yeux de mes dessins.

Je continue et les gens se pressent, regardent les dessins par-dessus les épaules de ceux qui sont juste devant eux. Ça rit. Ça ricane. Ça s'impatiente. Ils deviennent agressifs. Petit à petit, les reproches fusent. Un lecteur se plaint de sa dédicace, en réclame une autre. Un autre veut revendre son exemplaire. On me traite d'imposteur.

Au début, les gens sourient, essayent de bavarder avec moi, mais je n'arrive pas à leur répondre. Je transpire. Ma main tremble. J'ai peur qu'ils remarquent que mes dessins sont nuls.

Je voudrais fuir ou disparaître. Je ne peux pas. Je sais que le public a raison, que je ne sais pas dessiner, je voudrais pleurer mais je ne peux pas. Je n'existe pas. J'ai l'impression qu'ils vont me lyncher. Surgit quelqu'un qui me dit "Menteuse ! Judith Forest, ce n'est pas vous !..."

Momon
Thomas Boivin, William Henne
and Xavier Löwenthal ('Judith Forest'), 2011

strips about surreal periods of her life, satirical sex-changes and her epilepsy.

On the downside, in the search for the next *Maus* or *Persepolis*, success can breed formula, repetition and a graphic 'misery memoir' for every illness and world tragedy. Proliferating through the small press, webcomics and blogs, absolute beginners often start out by 'writing what they know', though not everyone's souvenirs or daily routine make for riveting reading. A backlash was inevitable. Vocal superhero fans who insisted on escapism and highly finished artwork dismissed the whole autobiography genre outright for its perceived dull navel-gazing. Creators, too, responded. In his 2002 tour-de-force *676 Apparitions of Killoffer*, the eponymous L'Association co-founder grew so frustrated with a commission to illustrate a trip abroad that he subverted it by accumulating the repeated versions he draws of himself on the page, like multiple ids and egos,

crowding him out of his apartment, creating a chaotic nightmare which climaxes in the 'original' Killoffer disposing of his rampant clones in a violent orgy. He later explained that this venting grew 'from a general exasperation with autobiographies. It was a period when too many had been crammed down our throats'.[6] In a rave review in the newspaper *Libération*, Dutch cartoonist and critic Willem hailed it as 'a graphic novel to end the autobiography craze and about time too!'

The 'craze' did not end there, of course. In 2009, an unknown debutante named Judith Forest received wide acclaim for her frank diary-form confessions in *1h25*, the journey time by rail between Paris and Brussels, during which she reflects on her problems with her parents, her drug addiction, sexual desires and emotional needs, incorporating several familiar faces from the Belgian art-comics scene. It ticked all the right boxes and the book took on a life of it own. The press and public lapped up *1h25* and it became by far the biggest seller to date from the normally quirky, experimental publishers 5e Couche. Forest gave interviews to the press and on radio and television, and built a following on social media and at comics festivals. But something was amiss. Her drawings looked too close to the style of one of her publishers, also a 5e Couche author. Her accounts in the book of meetings could not be corroborated by others supposedly present. In her 2010 sequel, *Momon* (p.101) she describes her increasing anxiety over the promotion of *1h25*, her solace in the arms of Fabrice Neaud, her nightmares of becoming invisible, her doubts about her role and very existence. Gradually, Judith Forest and the reader piece together proof that she is a fabrication, a 'J.F.' or jeune fille (the term for a 'young girl' in the lonely hearts classified ads), her graphic novel concocted by three men in only three days to exploit the expectations of the media and marketplace. In this meta-fiction, she becomes a self-aware figment who wonders, 'What if "sincerity" was nothing more than a sales strategy? And what if autobiography was the whore of literary genres?' *Momon* is slyly dedicated to 'all those people, and particularly the journalists, who allowed me to exist'.

If any book could 'end the autobiography craze', it should have been this cleverly calculated breach of the genre's implicit pact between author and reader. It poses uncomfortable questions about our desire for honesty, our gullibility and prurience, and how formulaic this genre

has become that such a persuasive narrator can be easily fabricated. In our age of reality TV, video diaries and Second Life, who do we trust? And we might ask, is *1h25* weaker for being fake? Seth's enquiry into a hitherto unacknowledged cartoonist named 'Kalo' in *It's A Good Life If You Don't Weaken* (1996) turned out to be pure fiction, but his themes of what makes an artist pursue their art or give up for an easier 'good life' ring true.

Despite all this, autobiography is not a craze or aberration; it has expanded the parameters and possibilities of comics. All of life can now be included in comics, where it's always belonged. Justin Green himself has made a return to the form he helped pioneer some forty years ago, this time portrayed by his wife Carol Tyler in her remarkable trilogy *You'll Never Know* (2009–12, right). In their 'thorny union', Green has been an addicted, unfaithful, absentee husband but their daughter's diagnosis of obsessive-compulsive disorder, like Green's, brings him back. A mixed-media scrapbook album in landscape format, Tyler's graphic memoir also focuses on her 'good and decent' father, a veteran bottling up eruptive memories of his part in the Second World War. Towards the end, Tyler shows her parents dancing together at a wedding to their song, for the last time, and realises, 'Certainly nobody in the crowd understood the significance of this moment or who they were. Some old couple. How could these kids know them? They'll never know them. Unless I try to explain, which is a good reason to write a book.' And a good reason to read one.

You'll Never Know Book 3: Soldier's Heart
Carol Tyler, 2012

THE HUMAN TOUCH:
STYLE AND INDIVIDUALITY

Fires
Lorenzo Mattotti, 1986

Mysteries and prejudices still surround the making of comics. It might surprise some, but comics do not come out of a sausage machine; they are the handiwork of human beings. The touch of their real or digital pencils, pens and brushes onto paper or into pixels, and the hand and mind behind them, are always there. Roy Lichtenstein is probably chiefly responsible for promulgating through his Pop art paintings the misconception that all American comic books, and so all comics, are drawn in the same standardised style, crudely coloured and poorly printed. His emphatic black outlines filled with layers of Benday dots in solid colours have come to define the popularly perceived 'comic book look', repeated ever since by designers, advertisers and comic artists themselves. In fact, Lichtenstein was never an 'Image Duplicator', to quote one of his paintings' ironic titles, itself a quote from comics dialogue. He would never duplicate panels extracted from comics exactly, line for line, partly because he was not that skilled a copyist, partly because he wanted to depersonalise and homogenise their imagery. In the end, he only ever approximated them.

On his Deconstructing Lichtenstein website, David Barsalou has identified many of the painter's original print sources and put them side by side with the subsequent canvases. Comparisons make it clear that Lichtenstein would re-draw and re-mix his samples and edit out numerous details and finesses in the original artwork, reducing the comics artists' variegated line weights,

brushstrokes and hatching techniques to a heavy-handed boldness. Fine lines in a woman's hair became thick masses, shading and depth effects became flattened. What the paintings gained in some simplified, poster-like impact, they lost in nuance and personality, as revealed in *WHAAT?*, Dave Gibbons' pointed reappropriation of Irv Novick's original panel on which Lichtenstein's *WHAAM!* was based (p.106). The mark-making of the human hand was buried or erased. Comics were not only anonymous, they were an industrialised product. Comics were sausages.

In many ways, those thirty-six-page war and romance anthologies which Lichtenstein would buy fresh off the newsstands for twelve cents in the early 1960s were churned out sausage-like on an assembly-line, meeting quotas and deadlines, making sales and profits. An editor at DC Comics would assign a writer's edited script to an artist, who would draw up the artwork on boards, usually fifty per cent larger ('half-up') or twice the size of the final printed page and starting in pencil, finishing in ink (sometimes done by another artist known as an 'inker'). Then a letterer would insert the balloons, captions, titles and sound effects, and a colourist would prepare a guide for the separators, often working by hand cutting up sheets of Benday dots, before thousands of copies were printed on absorbent newsprint and distributed. In the present, the technologies may have advanced but worldwide the pressures on creators in periodical commercial comics are as intense and relentless as ever. There

is little time here for much reflection or reconsideration; the idea of taking months or years to draft and re-draft one graphic novel is out of the question. It is all the more amazing how much good and sometimes amazing work can come out of this unforgiving system.

While searching through his comic books for inspiration, Lichtenstein could not have helped noticing how narrow a range of styles, storylines and stereotypes of the sexes their editors would accept. It was this conformity, applied to expressing the emotions of bloodless, macho combat, or romance from a typically blubbering, stuttering woman's perspective, which was ripe for his parodic exaggeration. The 1960s were dawning but the realities of the Vietnam war and women's changing roles went unnoticed at DC Comics. The industry leader insisted on a 'house' style for these genres and gave their writers and artists no credits, treating them as largely interchangeable and expendable. It would be the ranks of fandom, the community of studious collectors, whose eagle eyes for the distinguishing qualities and quirks of these mostly unsigned prolific draughtsmen, who would eventually identify and appreciate them.

Like most art forms and entertainments, comics are affected and afflicted by conformity, partly because certain artists prove so successful that they set the standard for a company, genre or era, until others come along and do the same. Success breeds excess. So after the dominance of elaborate rendering in Victorian illustration in Britain, Phil May and Tom Browne swept it away like a breath of fresh air with their lighter, cleaner approach, better suited to poor quality newsprint. While developing out of formative influences of their own, Osamu Tezuka, the 'God of Manga' in Japan, and Hergé and André Franquin in Belgium inspired schools of followers. Hergé's increasing fastidiousness became known as 'The Clear Line' for its clarity of drawing and storytelling, while ex-animator Franquin's panache inspired 'L'École Marcinelle' after the city of his publisher Dupuis. Both still exert a massive influence on Francophone *bandes dessinées* today. The drawing of certain characters could become their 'on-model' templates for many years for other artists. At Disney, the uncredited 'Good Duck' artist, later discovered by admirers to be Carl Barks, became the essential reference for generations of successors. During Marvel Comics' ascendency in the 1960s, artists were instructed to adapt their drawing to the distortions, foreshortening and dynamism of 'house artist' Jack Kirby. Spearheading the underground comix revolution in the mid- to late 1960s, Robert Crumb's artwork – itself a fusion from earlier humorous newspaper strips and comic books he idolised (including Barks) – became identified internationally with its times, to the point where artists as diverse as Swarte in the Netherlands, Jacques Tardi in France or Javier Mariscal in Spain all went through their foundational Crumb 'periods' in the early 1970s before branching off on their own paths.

A certain consistency to the drawing in a comic would seem to be essential,

because readers expect characters to look the same and be recognisable from panel to panel, a comic being of-a-piece by having what Thierry Groensteen has called 'iconic solidarity'.[1] This is also why publishers who own a 'legacy character' usually go to great efforts to replace the originating artist with another who can maintain it as closely as possible. On the other hand, deliberate contrasts or clashes of styles within the same comic can stir up intriguing effects. In Harvey Kurtzman's *Mad* comic book, two different artists drew his satire of George McManus's newspaper strip 'Bringing Up Father', about the down-to-earth Jiggs and his socially aspiring wife Maggie and their differing responses to sudden wealth and social climbing. Bill Elder mimics McManus's airy Art Deco elegance and slapstick played for laughs, but on alternate pages Bernie Krigstein illustrates the shadowy, 'serious' side of the domestic violence of Maggie's far-from-funny assaults on Jiggs with piles of dishes, rolling pins and worse. Here Jiggs is

drawn realistically, injured, concussed, bleeding, losing a tooth from these incessant knockabout routines which he always fails to escape. Jiggs becomes a character to be pitied, trapped in the 'same story again and again', who breaks the fourth wall and addresses the reader: 'That's right! Have a good laugh while my wife beats me up! Laugh like you have all these years!' In the final panel, suddenly drawn by Krigstein, Jiggs gets the last laugh by using his fortune to pay for some thuggish bodyguards. As always, Kurtzman's humorous stories go beyond parody to make a thought-provoking point.

This *Mad* story, drawn in 1954 by two very different artists, was a radical oddity in its day, but in recent years the counterpointing of styles has become a striking tool of graphic novelists. In 1994 in *The Tragical Comedy or Comical Tragedy of Mr Punch*, for example, by Neil Gaiman and Dave McKean, the usual expectations of photography to record reality and illustration to convey fantasy are reversed. McKean constructed and photographed elaborate puppets, sets, props and a theatre, reserving his drawings for the everyday scenes of the young boy and the puppeteer. This makes us question which of these worlds is the more 'real'. In *The Nao of Brown* (left), Glyn Dillon pencils his main narrative about Nao, a young half-Japanese woman plagued by violent, negative imaginings, with a light touch in watercolours. He interrupts this with an apparently unrelated, manga-inspired science fiction fantasy illustrated in tight ink and flat colours against black pages. These interludes come to be understood as Nao's favourite comic and animation and acquire an extra level of meaning as an allegorical commentary on her troubled self-esteem. At one critical point, these two storyworlds briefly collide to startling effect, as Nao's head becomes encased like a conker inside a huge spiny shell.

'Twin-tracked' narration is also applied by Joseph Lambert to *Annie Sullivan and the Trials of Helen Keller* (p.110). He shifts our attention back and forth between the exterior world of Sullivan's attempts to communicate with and educate the little girl Keller, who went blind and deaf aged only nineteen months, and Keller's interior world, how she sees, or imagines, herself, always in muted colours and engulfed by blackness. Initially, her self-image is blurry, an amorphous blank without features, but gradually, through sign language, she begins to know the names and concepts of people and objects. A sudden breakthrough in her understanding occurs when her teacher helps her make sense of water coming from a pump. The next morning, Lambert adds details to her inner self-portrait, showing her hair, and her two blind eyes waking and opening. The more she grasps of the world, the more her once-barren limbo fills with her representations and labels of them. Any such inconsistencies in style have typically been seen as problematic,

BELOW:
**Annie Sullivan and
the Trials of Helen Keller**
Joseph Lambert, 2012

RIGHT:
Rumble Strip
Woodrow Phoenix, 2008

shattering the illusion of a comic being the resolved creation of a single artist. In Hong Kong's high-volume martial art comics, however, no attempt is made to disguise the many hands at work, the style and medium altering from one panel or page to the next. Still, we expect that a realistic comic should be drawn realistically throughout, a humorous one humorously. But the mixing of more than one style is increasingly accepted. Japanese cartoonists like Shigeru Mizuki will naturally draw characters in a short-hand, caricatural way but place them within very detailed, realistic settings (p.109). What might seem disjointed to Western eyes seems to encourage manga readers to identify themselves more with the simplified characters and to share with them a richer sense of their surroundings. It has also become perfectly accepted for manga characters to shift in their representation, for example in moments of heightened emotion to transform temporarily into the 'chibi' style of a wild little infantilised figure, or sporting faces almost demonic with dark thoughts. The reader never loses track because enough of the character's distinguishing aspects, hair and clothes remain the same. In his relatively real-life tales of 'locas', delightfully crazy Hispanic-American women, Jaime Hernandez will sometimes switch a character into a she-devil, all snarling teeth and fuming with fury. Such momentary histrionic reactions, overblown like vaudeville, hark back to the roots of humorous comics.

An ever-expanding arsenal of co-existing styles of cartooning has amassed, to which contemporary comics creators can refer, with or without reverence, and whose associations can add extra levels for the knowledgeable reader. In *99 Ways To Tell A Story: Exercises in Style* (2005), Matt Madden demonstrates how diverse some of the possible approaches to the simplest of one-page, eight-panel comics can be. He quotes pre-existing styles from comics, including those of McCay, Herriman, Hergé, Kirby and Crumb. He references

YOUR CAR IS ITS OWN LITTLE ISLAND TOO.

WAITING FOR YOU SOMEWHERE OUT THERE IN THE MIDDLE OF THIS SEA OF SELF INVOLVED BUCCANEERS.

AND YOU WOULD LIKE TO REACH IT ALIVE.

THAT'S WHEN YOU BEGIN TO NOTICE THAT IN ALL THIS WIDESCREEN TARMAC FLATLAND THERE'S NOTHING TO PREVENT OTHER DRIVERS INADVERTENTLY KILLING YOU EXCEPT SOME STRIPS OF PAINT.

AND YOU HAVE TO ADMIT THAT DOESN'T FEEL LIKE QUITE ENOUGH PROTECTION.

genre tropes such as war and romance and the conventions of daily newspaper strips, comics-format religious tracts or public service announcements, but also sets himself all sorts of formal constraints – narrating only in close-ups, silhouettes or sound effects. As Madden asks in his introduction, 'Can a story, however simple or mundane, be separated from the manner is which it is told?' He concludes: 'It's clear that what appear to be merely "stylistic" choices are in fact an essential part of the story.'

Madden's experiments suggest that substance is inseparable from style. To give one example, before commencing his 2008 graphic novel *Rumble Strip* (p.111) Woodrow Phoenix made some radical stylistic decisions crucial to his project's impact. His intention was to interrogate our indifference towards traffic 'accidents' which kill millions of us every year, but are somehow seen as acceptable collateral losses for the right to drive. Phoenix is not opposed to cars – he enjoys driving himself – but he wanted to respond to the loss of his younger sister who as a child had been struck and killed by a car. He deliberately chose to avoid limiting the scope of his narrative to a heartstring-tugging autobiography. To his mind, 'it was more effective to weave my personal stories into the mix of experiences for a richer and more representative text that could cover a lot more ground. Expansive, not reductive. I wanted the reader to think about what happens in and around a car. The best way to do that was to literally put them in the "driving seat". And in the pedestrian's shoes.'[2]

One problem with the comics medium is that it usually presents us with a clear protagonist – visibly male or female, young or old, of a certain appearance or race – who may not represent the reader and who we may not warm to. Phoenix avoids this specificity and exclusion by showing nobody, and having us 'see' through the eyes of an unseen car driver and pedestrian. As in many computer games, the reader-player becomes the actor. This completely subjective viewpoint is rare in comics, because so many of them are built around active leading characters. The only human beings Phoenix presents in the book are their symbolic representations familiar from street signs and road markings. Miles of empty motorways and car parks recall the fantasies of advertisements, which show no other cars but the one being promoted, speeding along the open road alone. The very absence of people draws attention to them and to how a driver, enclosed in his or her own bubble environment, can become separated from others. From inside that head, looking through the windscreen, we cannot avoid seeing and reading Phoenix's polemic in captions overlaid emphatically centre-stage, as if they have taken the place normally occupied by the hero. The black-and-white artwork may look cold and diagrammatic, recalling the Highway Code, or certain unpeopled Lichtenstein paintings, but Phoenix consciously avoided digital solutions in favour of drawing and inking entirely by hand.

It is becoming clear that there is no reason why all the pages or protagonists in a comic should be illustrated in a uniform manner. Mixing and contrasting techniques are opening up fresh avenues of expression for graphic novelists. In *Don't Go Where I Can't Follow* (2006), Anders Nilsen compiles a heartfelt memoir of his relationship with his fiancée, Cheryl Weaver, who died of Hodgkin's lymphoma. He narrates not only in comics, but also in sections of tender postcards they exchanged, the journal he wrote on lined paper torn from a notebook, photographs and souvenirs, and drawings of her final days and her memorial. Dominique Goblet in *Faire semblant c'est mentir* (2007) evokes anxieties about her childhood and a broken romance, co-written with her ex-lover, through a variety of media from fragile, childlike pencil drawings to feverishly cross-hatched oil paintings, always appropriate to her feelings. Deconstructing his previous autobiographical oeuvre, Eddie Campbell goes missing in *The Fate of the Artist* (2006), leaving him free to mingle six different threads, each stylistically and typographically distinct, including a detective's thwarted attempts to trace the absent author and clippings from invented Sunday pages of a humorous newspaper strip. As fragmentary and fractured as these threads become, connections soon start to spark between them.

Few have experimented as far with this interplay as David Mazzucchelli, who gives each of his main characters in *Asterios Polyp* (p.114) not only their own signature graphic style, like a leitmotiv, but also distinct typography for their speech and specific shapes for their balloons. So, arrogant architect Asterios Polyp holds forth in emphatic sans serif capitals inside rectangular blocks, while Hana, his Japanese girlfriend, speaks in a softer voice, evoked through a cursive upper-and-lower case within curvaceous bubbles. When the couple first meet at a party, they and everyone else are drawn in wildly varied styles. Asterios comes in cool cobalt and is made up of cylinders, spheres and other Aristotelian outlines, while Hana in warm magenta appears like a carved statuette in textured volume. As the two of them start to get on, they take on each other's distinctive visual register, literally coming together and harmonising, as do the furniture and room around them. Later, when they argue, they revert to their separate styles.

Mazzucchelli's method is a prime example of illustrators of other people's scripts branching out on their own, taking baby steps with manageable short stories, but eventually finding their feet and achieving a magnum opus. Numerous examples – Barry Windsor-Smith, Enki Bilal, Frank Miller, Mike Mignola, Jill Thompson, Linda Medley and David Lapham – show that this can be liberating and transforming. After years of drawing the western adventures of Lieutenant Blueberry, Jean Giraud revived an earlier pen-name, Moebius, to explore personal passions. His last self-published solo work, *Inside Moebius*, shows him at his most free, newly inspired after giving up drugs (p.118). He lets loose his different incarnations, such as his hippy rebel self from the 1970s or his recent self, older if not wiser, to mingle with the

AND WHEN HE CAME OVER TO INTRODUCE HIMSELF,

I'M SORRY. MY NAME'S ASTERIOS POLYP.

SHE FELT SHE WAS STARING STRAIGHT INTO THE SPOTLIGHT.

cowboy Blueberry, with Moebius's own science fiction characters, and even with Osama bin Laden, thrown together in a desert that could be as much the Wild West as another planet. Each a facet of his personality, the characters interact. His thoughts unravel in playful improvisation and meditation as he draws and writes without preparation, putting ink straight onto the page.

There is an argument that the best comics creations come from one person who can determine the whole complex alchemy of the verbal and visual. Contradicting this, there have been plenty of outstanding partnerships, who prove more than the sum of their parts and have forged a true meeting of minds: Pierre Christin and Jean-Claude Mezières on the seminal science fiction saga *Valerian*; Kazuo Koike and Goseki Kojima on the rogue samurai epic *Lone Wolf and Cub*; Alan Moore and David Lloyd on the masked anarchist *V for Vendetta*. In many countries, the old editorial systems divided up the workload to maximise output. They kept authors and illustrators largely apart to divide and rule. An artist would not be involved until a finished script was approved. Fortunately, writers today can communicate with their collaborators to bring out the best in them, sometimes sketching small, loose 'thumbnails', and knowing when to let the pictures do the telling.

Problems can arise, though, if such scripts seek only to ape a screenplay. In the view of another artist-turned-writer, Seth, it is inappropriate to connect comics to film, or to prose,

and better to see them as a mixture of poetry and graphic design. 'The poetry connection is more appropriate because of both the condensing of words and the emphasis on rhythm. Comic book artists have for a long time connected themselves to film, but in doing so, have reduced their art to being merely a 'storyboard' approach.'[3] Instead of striving for a movie's photographed veneer of verisimilitude, Seth believes, 'the drawings in a comic are generally memory-drawings; the simplicity of the ink lines can act as a memory trigger. The reader/viewer ideally is a ghost floating over a dream world of memory. The cartoonist is trying to boil down real life experience into an image that is capable of conveying the depth of life by only suggesting it.'

Part of the problem with many comics is their graphic directness. Everything is there for all to see. Flashy hyperbole and bombast may suit the art for certain heroic and fantasy genres, and extreme facial exaggerations may hammer home melodrama or humour, but they can obliterate the subtler power of suggestion. All too often, instead of 'less is more', it becomes 'more is not enough'. After the collapse of 1960s Batmania, upcoming artist Neal Adams imported photo-referenced pseudo-realism from soap opera-style newspaper strips and advertising art to undo the camp garishness of the Batman television show and reverse the comic books' declining sales. Under Adams's influence, superheroes increasingly emoted with anguished faces and gritted teeth and their bodies became over-idealised anatomy drawings. This

Asterios Polyp
David Mazzucchelli, 2009

push towards a heightened 'realism' culminated in the fully painted panels by Alex Ross, the Norman Rockwell of American superheroics, whose accomplished portrayals resemble the characters' CGI-enhanced appearances on the big and small screen. Chris Ware's approach could not be more different. He tends to avoid showing his iconically refined characters facing front and bursting with emotion. Ware prefers to have them turn their heads away, or be seen from behind or partially cropped, leaving their feelings to the reader's imagination. Rather than playing up dramatic turning-points, he will consign these to small panels, defusing them. Ware's version of Superman is balding, overweight and mean-spirited, leaping from a tall building and falling to his death, depicted from a cool distance and in silence. As Ivan Brunetti advises in his course book *Cartooning*, 'If we are to aim for subtlety and complexity, we must "turn down the volume" and discern how much can be communicated before we add the extra layer of words.'

There are various methods for learning how to make comics. Many artists are self-taught, or start out that way by copying their favourites. The danger is that you never get to be yourself. American cartoonist Jules Feiffer recalls his teenage aspirations: 'Unwittingly, believing with all my heart that this was progress, I began to divest myself of myself ... I didn't use my betters as reference points to build a style of my own. No, I stole their drawings, line for line, fold for fold, shadow for shadow. And the more I distanced myself from what made me love being a cartoonist

in the first place, the more professional I thought I was.'[4] It can help a career to start working as the humblest assistant to a 'master artist' and learn on the job. More by luck and persistence than talent, young Feiffer was taken on in the 1940s in Will Eisner's crowded 'sweatshop', packaging comics piecemeal for client publishers. Poor pay and conditions and his ineptitude at most tasks could not dampen Feiffer's thrill at living his dream of working in comics. He would eventually turn his strengths and weaknesses into his unique satirical voice.

Later, Wally Wood joined Eisner's staff on 'The Spirit' and based on this, would set up his own studio and hire assistants to speed up his sometimes sluggish production. Wood's semi-joking motto, hung in a frame on his studio wall, advised: 'Never draw anything you can copy, never copy anything you can trace, never trace anything you can cut out and paste up.' Wood also sketched '22 panels that always work!!', a reminder as much for himself as his assistants to get the story drawn and not to waste time 'noodling'. The panels' assorted compositions, angles and lighting were intended to provide 'some interesting ways to get some variety into those boring panels where some dumb writer has a bunch of lame characters sitting around and talking for page after page!'

The hard graft of meeting regular deadlines in this often solitary profession was a far cry from the glamorous lifestyle promised in advertisements for cartooning courses and trade schools. The advert for the

Le Dieu du 12
Alex Barbier, 1982

Escuela Panamericana in Buenos Aires, Argentina, showed a good-looking cartoonist, always male, relaxing by his swimming pool sipping cocktails, surrounded by female admirers. Nevertheless, outstanding creators like Alberto Breccia and Hugo Pratt taught there and could pass on their wisdom to students, among them the future greats José Muñoz and Oscar Zarate. Similarly, in New York in 1947, Burne Hogarth, famed for his lavish Sunday pages of 'Tarzan', co-founded The School of Visual Arts (SVA) to train students, often demobbed military men using their GI Bill money, to enter the industrial side of the medium. Amongst them was 'Spider-Man' co-creator Steve Ditko. Later, Eisner, Kurtzman and Spiegelman would also teach there, encouraging such wayward talents as Mark Newgarden, Kaz, Peter Bagge, Daniel Clowes and Drew Friedman, who quipped that the SVA was 'one step above clown college'. Schools specifically for comics art, and modules and degrees within art colleges, have multiplied around the world. The risk

remains that, to forge a career, pupils taught by working professionals will repeat their tics and tricks or adhere to the conventions of the industry. Fortunately, there are tutors who want to bring out their students' individuality, and a greater diversity of styles, media and contents than ever before is being accepted by publishers and the public.

For decades, due mainly to the economies and limitations of printing, comics have been dominated by the inked, black line, ideal for crisp reproduction. The chance to paint comics in colour without solid outlines became possible once improved print technology became more available and affordable. Photogravure presses enabled 'Dan Dare' in *Eagle* in 1950 to present a dazzling, convincing window into the future during Britain's drab, post-war recovery. To supply two pages every week, Frank Hampson devised an elaborate process requiring a team of assistants who worked from photographs of props and family and friends modelling in costume. British

into the graphic novel (p.105). Calling on her Madagascan roots, Armella Leung sculpted her panels in clay to resemble wood carvings and hid some characters behind African masks to represent the social masks their roles demand (left). In *The Black Project* (pp.120–1), Gareth Brookes juxtaposes linocut prints with embroidery, appropriate mixed media for his tale of a shy young man who crafts D.I.Y. girlfriends out of household objects.

Tensions between conformity and individuality in comics will never go away. Brunetti warns about forcing a certain style onto one's artwork, rather than letting it 'grow of its own volition, from the totality of our influences and abilities (or inabilities, as the case may be). When style is not the natural outcome, the outgrowth, of all these things, we have instead a repugnant, off-putting mannerism.' Ronald Searle reflected on where individuality comes from in a letter to his friend, animator Uli Meyer, dated 29 August 2009: 'Actually I think the whole secret of drawing is looking and then interpreting. Looking at what is in front of you, or what is in your head. (I never put my pen to paper until I see a clear image in my head and forget the pen, which is only a technicality anyway.) If one simply draws without adding yourself – your own vision – to the subject, the results are inevitably clichés and empty. This is all done at a million miles a second as the subject passes through the eye and around the brain to come down to the fingers. But individuality is attached on the way! Which is the marvel.'

children's weekly comics led the way in the 1950s by allowing artists like Frank Bellamy and Ron Embleton to craft such vibrant, fully painted comics printed on quality paper. In America, Harvey Kurtzman and his cohorts started their 'Little Annie Fanny' adult satires in 1962 to take advantage of *Playboy*'s budget and glossy printing. They were followed later in the 1960s in the underground movement by Richard Corben, who pioneered a lush, three-dimensional physicality through his own complex, hand-made method of colour separations. Among the innovators of 'direct colour' in French comics was painter and former art teacher Alex Barbier, debuting in *Charlie Mensuel* in 1975, with his William Burroughs-inspired experiments in sensuous, translucent watercolours (p.117). Another transformation was *Fires* (1986) by the Italian artist Lorenzo Mattotti, who demonstrated the narrative and emotional potential of incorporating techniques and palettes from Expressionism and Fauvism

OVERLEAF:
The Black Project
Gareth Brookes, 2013
Original artwork

I had to think of a way to make Melissa some legs and arms. Watching a programme on BBC 2 about Iron Age Britain gave me a good idea.

In the programme it showed how Iron Age people wove baskets out of bulrushes.

INFINITE CANVASES:
COMICS IN THE DIGITAL AGE

Few developments have democratised and globalised the creation, distribution and consumption of comics so powerfully as the internet. The medium is no longer dependent on publishers commissioning creators, printing their work in ink on paper, stapling or binding them into magazines and books, sending out quantities to distributors to supply retailers, hopefully to be bought by the general public. The internet has changed this convoluted system and cut out many, if not all, of its middle-men. Creators and readers are more directly in touch than ever, all over the world. For more and more people, making and reading comics means making and reading them electronically, as pixels replace pen and ink, and screens replace paper. Each new technology and platform triggers innovations and challenges in what comics can offer. Simpler, single-strip gag comics seem better suited to the small screen sizes of mobile phones than the larger pages of comic books and graphic novels. Something in the experience of comics across the page and the spread is definitely lost when screen space allows you to take in only one panel at a time. Intriguingly, in Japan, one genre of manga that has proved particularly profitable on mobile phones is 'yaoi', homoerotic romances between idealised men created by and for women, because readers who felt embarrassed buying the printed books could purchase these stories discreetly for their phone and would not share them with other women. Larger, lightweight colour screens on portable e-book readers and tablets, notably the iPad, are transforming comics again,

making them more responsive and interactive, literally at our fingertips. Drawing, in all its subtleties, is becoming more 'telegenic' on screen, no longer a victim to lo-res pixellation but crystal clear in high definition.

Comics have been part of the digital revolution from the beginning, before the dawn of the World Wide Web and mobile phones. In the days of CompuServe in the 1980s, for example, American cartoonist Eric Monster Millikin was quick to seize on the chance to disseminate his comics via online file transfers. From the age of eleven in 1985, Millikin began 'Witches and Stitches', his satire of *The Wizard of Oz*, about a love triangle between the Scarecrow and two witches, using digital delivery to circumvent censorship. The internet soon beckoned. 'In the early Nineties, it was the natural thing to do to start putting my art on the web as soon as I first got my hands on a browser.'[1] Millikin was not alone. Some early American webtoonists borrowed their college's computer access to produce and post their comics, but once home computing and laptops caught on, the online comics revolution became unstoppable. Initially, the short, horizontal newspaper-strip format suited the screen width, offering easy-to-read, stand-alone jokes without the need to scroll.

The internet can serve as a forum for low-cost promotion and audience development, and substantial funding for self-publishing through Kickstarter, Indiegogo and other crowd-sourcing systems. It also provides the incentive

Shooting War
Internet and print versions
Anthony Lappé (writer) and Dan Goldman
(artist), 2006 and 2008

to supply a new instalment every day or week. A number of significant autobiographical printed comics might well have never flourished without the support of their original online readerships. In 'Mom's Cancer' (below) Brian Fies shared his family's realities with a community hungry both for information they weren't getting from the medical profession, and for a connection with someone going through similar crises. When Darryl Cunningham began posting his experiences as a psychiatric nurse, he received such positive feedback, it motivated him to pursue his 'Psychiatric Tales' and helped him realise their therapeutic value, to him and to others. For over fourteen years, starting in October 1998, James Kochalka was the first to post a daily diary comic, recording some moment from his day in a compact, square, two-by-two panel strip called 'American Elf'.

Blogs by cartoonists have proliferated in France, leading to numerous 'free-form'

journals, such as Lewis Trondheim's 'Little Nothings' (right) and Boulet's 'Notes', as well as to successful work by young women such as Margaux Motin and Penelope Bagieu, self-commentators speaking to their generation in chic and sassy satires. Rumours abound about which famous male cartoonists lurk behind the pen-name 'Frantico', whose celibate, sex-obsessed confessions on a blog in 2005 became a hilarious best-selling book.

Just as previous technological advances such as cheap photocopying empowered novices to try their hand at making comics, so the relatively low cost of producing webcomics has opened the medium to newcomers for play and experimentation. South Korea has been at the forefront of a form of webcomic or 'webtoon' which unfolds not in individual black-and-white pages like a typical Korean comic or *manhwa*, but panel by panel, separated onto one long, vertically scrolling page per chapter, and usually in colour. Widespread internet

click through smoothly from one page to the next. As a result, the shape and dynamics of the page have altered and there has been a subsequent increase in book compilations using this format. The internet has been invaluable as a way, above all for creators, to develop ambitious projects without relinquishing their ownership, to serialise new episodes daily, weekly or regularly, offer sample extracts, learn from reader feedback and nurture a faithful audience. Remarkably, even if an entire series is available online for free, it has been found that plenty of readers still want to own it in a tangible printed edition.

A webcomic itself can generate an income and even a living. Since 1998, hard-working British pioneer John Allison has cultivated a supportive following for his entertaining serials, all set in the fictional West Yorkshire town of Tackleford, and he has carved out a solo cottage industry via mail order, exhibiting at fairs and festivals and offering subscriptions, commissions, T-shirts, prints, book collections and tea towels. After more than seven years of the supernatural humour of 'Scary Go Round', in 2009 Allison jumped ahead three years to relate the school mysteries of 'Bad Machinery', switching to four episodes a week in a landscape format.

Like many more traditionalist webcomics creators, Allison eschews fancy bells and whistles and sticks to the equivalent of a printed page. Others embrace the additional reading tools and experiences which technology

access across the country has given millions easy access to these regular episodes for free via portal sites such as Daum (2003) and Naver (2005). Because they are less subject to publishers' demands, Korean webtoonists can work with more personal styles and subjects, from slice-of-life and topical comedies to chillers like 'Apartment' by Kang Full, whose untrained, simplified cartooning succeeds in stoking the tension as you scroll down the page. Another secret to these webtoons' success is the communal online feedback from readers who become attached to the characters.

Elsewhere, many webcomics creators have adapted to the standard landscape 16:9 ratio of a computer monitor and stick to the screen area easily visible 'above the fold' to allow readers to

ABOVE:
Little Nothings
Lewis Trondheim, 2007

LEFT:
Mom's Cancer
Brian Fies, 2004

allows. In the case of the historical supernatural thriller 'Valentine' by Alex de Campi and Christine Larsen, enthusiastic readers have translated the texts, dropped in over the artwork, into fourteen languages. De Campi and Larsen are not alone in abandoning the traditional multi-panel page of comics in favour of single panels that fill the screen format and progress, on the reader's click, mostly through dissolves and sometimes by panning across a wider scene. Another innovation, for example in Dan Goldman's smart paranormal parody of the Miami real-estate business, 'Red Light Apartments', is to maintain a series of whole landscape comics pages which readers can zoom into and move around for themselves, but to offer an optional 'Guided View' which superimposes a reading order, closing in on each panel and tracking across it and across each page. This focusing and direction is especially handy for readers not accustomed to navigating through the whole comics page, which remains visible on screen as a slightly blurred backdrop, just one click away.

In 2006, three years into the Iraq War, Goldman started working with journalist Anthony Lappé on a hard-hitting, darkly humorous projection of America's entanglements in the Middle East, set in 2011, ten years after '9/11', and entitled 'Shooting War' (p.123). A cocky anti-corporate video blogger is signed up by a ratings-hungry global news network and embedded within an army unit in Baghdad. The reports he sends back blow the lid off the escalating extremisim on both sides of

the 'War on Terror'. Goldman and Lappé began by previewing eleven chapters on the online personal storytelling magazine *SMITH*, reaching a web-savvy audience that was more familiar with films, television, games and magazines than comics. As the story is set somewhere between real-world headlines and brand-names and a meta-fictional near-future, Goldman created a suitably lurid, hyperrealist style of live newscasting by blending vector drawing, digital painting, collage, graphic design and photography, integrating actual news sources, including the Defense Department's own photo reportage from Iraq, and applying motion blurring and other effects to turn each panel into its own self-contained reality. Goldman and Lappé took advantage of the internet to incorporate voiceover narration, genuine frontline audio clips, Flash animation and other convincing simulacra. Their cocktail of government exposés, media celebrity, robotic warfare and cross-cultural romance hooked a viewership eager for *SMITH*'s weekly update, and secured them a deal in 2007 for the revised and expanded print graphic novel which they had always intended.

SMITH went on to commission another news-based webcomic from Josh Neufeld, whose blog and subsequent book recorded his experiences as a Red Cross volunteer during the aftermath of Hurricane Katrina in New Orleans in 2005. For 'A.D.: New Orleans After the Deluge', Neufeld went back and settled on six people as 'characters' whose stories he would tell. As well as a blog and resource list, each monthly

Dear Patagonia
Samples from App version
Jorge González, 2012

Dear PATAGONIA

AÓNIK'ENK

chapter came with hyperlinks beneath certain panels, for example to video interviews he had conducted with the survivors. As Neufeld told *SMITH*, 'Because *A.D.* depicts real people, places, and events, it's possible to link relevant items in scenes we depict here, which we believe amplifies the reader experience. When [one featured couple] Leo and Michelle are driving out of the city, for example, the reader can click on a link to view a YouTube video of the evacuation.'[2] Similarly, on the app version of Jorge Gonzalez's *Dear Patagonia*, layers of extra material, from his research to his artistic process, deepen the appreciation of his graphic novel. The single linear trajectory of a story is being reconfigured by providing readers with links to background information, but perhaps at the risk of distracting them from their immersive involvement with the main narrative.

The interactivity and multi-modality of digital comics have led to the notion of the reader not only having control of the reading experience of a comic, but also having a choice of more than one path to follow. Stories no longer have to be linear, with a single beginning, middle and end, but can divide and deviate with wildly differing trajectories and conclusions. As early as 1963, far-sighted American information technology pioneer Ted Nelson had coined the concepts of 'hypertext' and 'hypermedia', publishing them in 1965. In a paper five years later, Nelson proposed the 'hyper-comic' as a potential screen-based educational tool which 'branches on the student's request. For instance, different characters could be used to

explain things in different ways, with the student able to choose which type of explanation he wanted at a specific time.' Nelson's predictions would take some time and adjustments before coming to fruition. Before the internet, prototype hypercomics came in printed form as offshoots of role-playing and 'Choose Your Own Adventure' books such as *2000AD*'s spin-off magazine *Dice Man* in 1986, reaching its zenith in the satirical 'dole-playing' graphic novel *You Are Maggie Thatcher* by Pat Mills and Hunt Emerson. For a while, the CD-Rom fad seemed to offer a solution, but hypercomics were eventually realized above all as an evolution from experimental webcomics.

In 1996, Dave McKean and programmer Chris Miller took some significant small steps and giant leaps with Club Salsa (right), a website for the New Media department of American advertising and public relations agency Karakas, VanSickle, Ouellette. Their purpose was to deliver 'product information, online customer forums and ongoing serial entertainment built around twenty-four murder-mystery episodes that will unfold throughout the next year.' Set in a cyberpunk nightclub whose clients ingest 'Read Only chilies' to enter virtual realities, its cool credentials led to Netscape using the site to demonstrate its latest Navigator browser. At the time, McKean explained, 'Telling stories on the net (or any of the variety of multimedia currently evolving) is a troublesome task. Actually, I think multimedia is not the place for linear narrative, but that's a different soapbox. At least with this biweekly updated story, the linear

Club Salsa
Menu and extracts from Chapters 1 and 2
Dave McKean, 1996

And you did manage to convince our nice mr. Lizard of the purity of our drinks in this establishment.

As we watch our ill-fated friend take his final sip...

You must be wondering why?

What a senseless waste of virtuality you must be thinking.

Why introduce such unnecessary nastiness into our innocuous leisure activities?

If you've quite finished?

I will have to ask you to cool your nerves, my friend.

Not only are you drawing rather too much attention to yourself.

Not only have you destroyed some extremely rare and expensive merchandise.

But our friend, the Gecko King...

... only drinks water!

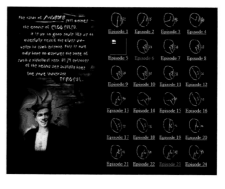

nature of the narrative is retained. There are a few choices for the viewer to make: which room to visit next, how the pieces of time fit together. But like all good stories, most of the interactivity takes place in your head. It's up to you to piece the jigsaw together.'[3]

The new millennium ushered in a significant expansion in how comics might operate on the internet with Scott McCloud's insight in *Reinventing Comics* in 2000 that 'the monitor which so often acts as a page may also act as a window'.[4] McCloud envisaged the potential of comics breaking free from the strictures of paper and print, from the regular rhythmic pagination, from identical units of a relatively modest grouping of panels. Nor was there a need any longer for the dimensions of a comic to be defined and confined by the edges of a computer screen. Now they could mutate beyond them into stranger, unpredictable configurations, akin to networks, subway systems, flow-charts, maps, atomic structures, puzzles or mazes, traversable along multiple trails. With the screen as a directional porthole or spyglass, McCloud called on creators to reimagine the internet as an 'infinite canvas'. McCloud practised what he preached with 'Choose Your Own Carl' in 2001, inviting readers to suggest variations on Carl, the unlucky character he had introduced in his theoretical book *Understanding Comics* in 1993. Carl's doom always begins with a promise and ends with his gravestone.

Another American cartoonist, Jason Shiga, adapted his self-published hypercomic print project *Meanwhile*

(p.133) for the web, allowing readers at certain key junctures to select from two or more directions in which to continue the story by following panels connected with small plugs. A subsequent graphic novel version resorted to index tags along the vertical outer edges of the pages to direct readers, but its ideal format, released in 2012 for iPad, orientates readers by displaying the entire intricate layout so they can zoom in and out of it, backtracking easily to try another pathway. This sort of zooming interface had been pioneered in 2002 by British webcomic creator Daniel Merlin Goodbrey, making the hypercomic's spatial map easily viewable and navigable for the first time.

Experimentation of this sort was rife around the turn of twenty-first century. In France, some members of L'Association joined other practitioners and theorists to explore how adding formal constraints would affect the creation and expression of comics, forming the 'Ouvroir de Bande Dessinée Potentielle', as the comics counterpart to the literary workshop OuLiPo founded in 1960 by Raymond Queneau and François Le Lionnais. As one example of an OuBaPo 'generative' constraint, Killoffer's print piece 'Acrostic' presents a mere sixteen panels in four rows of four which offer a plethora of stories by being read horizontally, vertically or at random. As OuBaPo's translator and American correspondent Matt Madden observed, 'This comic gives a sense of the poetic potential of an open-ended intermingling of images and phrases.'[5] So too does Antony Johnston and Ben Templesmith's 2001 online hypercomic

After Days of Passion, whose twelve scrawled icons – a wallet, a beer bottle, a syringe of drugs, a letter, a bottle of pills, a blaze, a staring eye, a couple arguing, an ashtray, a bed, a door, a house – offer the reader different steps to lose themselves inside the narrator's constant bleak ruminations, It is 'a collage piece, with no arbitrary narrative structure, inviting the reader to piece together parts of the puzzle themselves, through fragments and shreds of the whole, presented as a montage of illustration and text.'[6] For his ongoing webcomic 'xkcd', Randall Munroe makes up for rudimentary art chops with clever concepts. In 'Click and Drag', his stick-figure hero floats up holding a balloon and ponders: 'From the stories I expected the world to be sad and it was. And I expected it to be wonderful. It was. I just didn't expect it to be so big.' To convey vastness, Munroe concocted a gigantic panel to 'click and drag' across, packed with sight gags and geek culture references. It wasn't long before other programmers took to re-coding it to make it simpler to explore. This panel, if printed out, was estimated as 46 feet wide, surely the largest yet. Though this is not strictly sequential, Munroe suggests a coda on the far right of the panel, where his balloon kid speculates aloft: 'I wonder where I'll float next'. Webcomics like these can take us anywhere.

Another wide-open space for multi-cursal comics was provided by the white cube of the art gallery. Comics art conceived for print had been framed and exhibited in galleries and museums before, supplemented by a lucrative commercial market of specialist dealers catering to collectors. Gallery comics are works made specifically for exhibition and not necessarily for publication, such as OuBaPo member Étienne Lécroart's ludic constructs of comics whose stories change as the reader turns their hinged panels (above). Another influential gallery for comics was conceived in Turin in 2000 by Swedish artist Lars Arrhenius at the first Biennale Internazionale Arte Giovane. Along all four walls of a gallery, he organised 170 square wordless prints of 'The Man Without One Way', showing a man walking forwards from left to right, his main horizontal narrative frequently deviating into alternative narratives above or below, growing from each encounter, each door, each decision he takes, representing some of the myriad possibilities every moment brings. As with the internet's zooming interface, the visitor could scope out the overall project by looking from a distance around the gallery and then choose where to enter the sequences close up.

Arrhenius's system of a horizontal main story forming a 'spine', out of which could branch many other scenarios, was developed by Tom Gauld, Brad Brooks and myself in 2003 for the inaugural Comica Festival at London's Institute of Contemporary Arts. Stretching to seventeen metres along the Concourse Gallery's continuous wall, 'PoCom' (short for Potential Comic, a nod to OuBaPo) was structured around the spine of Gauld's skit of a man going out to buy milk, presented in thirty-eight larger panels printed on yellow paper to resemble Post-It notes. Gauld co-

Planches en vrac ou à la découpe
With moveable hinged panels
Étienne Lécroart, 2011

operated with seventeen other artists to introduce into his panels their choice of character or element as a springboard or climax for their playful branching stories on smaller squares of yellow paper. Among them was Goodbrey, who refined his zooming Infinite Canvas delivery system into 'The Tarquin Engine' for PoCom's online version, allowing a smooth bouncing rhythm to the reading and four clickable stages of blow-ups, from an unreadable distant overview of it all to the enlargement of each panel of the subsidiary stories. The originators' ambition, still to be realised, is to extend PoCom around another three walls of a gallery and then connect panels with further stories across the floor and ceiling, and cutting diagonally across the gallery space, to burst out beyond this cube to create a blossoming organic nest of stories, achievable only in virtual space. In Goodbrey's latest site-specific hypercomic, *Black Hats In Hell* (p.137), he positions the reader inside a gunfight, between the two cowboys' synchronous points of view shown on opposite walls. Elsewhere, he uses a corner like a page turn to add time between panels, or reconfigures them to mimic the actions within them.

To address the problems which the three-dimensional physical space of the gallery presents for showcasing comics, Dave McKean was one of four artists invited by me to devise a hypercomic as a site-specific installation for the exhibition *Hypercomics: The Shape of Comics To Come* in 2010 at the Pumphouse Gallery in London's Battersea Park. To respond to the one constraint – that the story must relate

to the gallery location – McKean tapped into a memory of an assault in a park, which he retold from three viewpoints, that of the attacker, the victim and a witness. He also referred to the park's former deer enclosure by incorporating fiercely competitive stags to symbolise the three males involved. His title, 'The Rut', reflects this aggression, and its sexual connotations, as well as the idea of being 'stuck in a rut', unable to move on from the trauma (p.135). After the scene-setting introduction, the visitor followed each of the three versions of the assault, whose panels split away to fill the gallery space, trailing vertically and overhead or across the floor. In the middle of the room, the public could get another triple perspective, this time reflecting on the incident with hindsight. By peering through three different red, antler-topped masks, they literally occupied the headspace of each of the trio. Each person's mask was aligned to bring into focus the fractured text and images of their worldview painted onto a large white trunk. McKean filled the walls with three enlarged photographs of stone heads, symbolically cracked and crumbling, and with a soft-sculpture body, presumably the victim's, again with antlers, prostrate over branches and secreted behind one wall. With a trio of unreliable narrators and no instructions or set order, visitors were left to their own devices. Similarly, some of the 3D comics conceived by contemporary Finnish comics artists for the exhibition *Eyeballing! The New Forms of Comics* in 2012 at Kiasma, Helsinki's Museum of Contemporary Art, hint at the exciting possibilities for 'gallery comics' unleashed from the page.

Meanwhile
App version
Jason Shiga, 2001–11

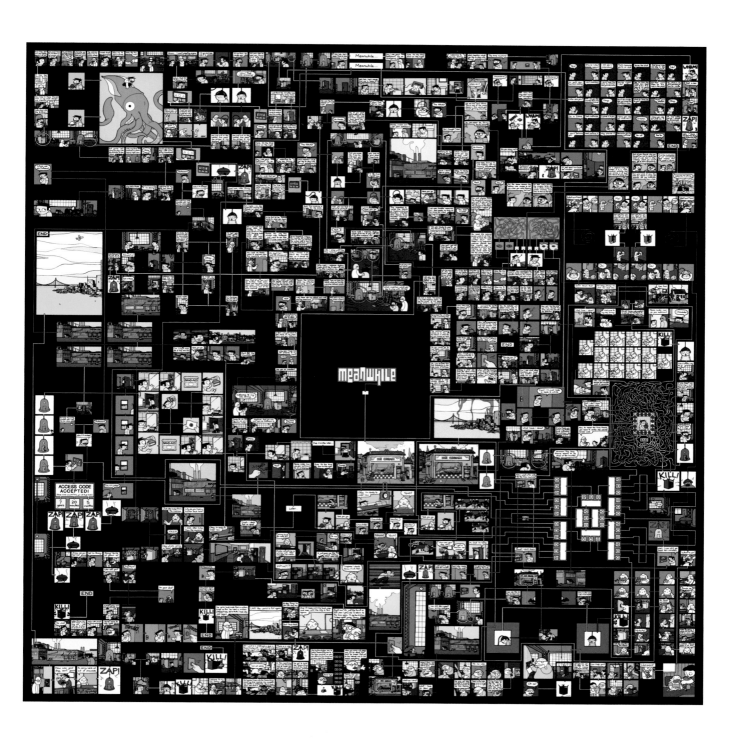

Other new digital forms of comics call into question the nature of the medium's specificity. Touch screens make activation more immediate, no longer scrolling or clicking cursors or buttons. Swiping and other gestures intuitive to iPad and tablet users add fresh ways to interact with the comics page. Sound in comics is not always disruptive. The addition of a purely ambient soundtrack, for example in Cognito Comics' documentary exposé *CIA: Operation Ajax* (2011), still leaves the reader in control of when to move on to read the next panel. The prologue to Ryan Woodward's futuristic baseball fantasy 'Bottom of the Ninth' (2012) gives the choice of reading and/or listening to the dialogue, while inserting short flourishes of animation in several panels. In *La Douce* (p.136), François Schuiten's tribute to Belgian steam locomotives, readers can download 'augmented reality' software to activate 3D-animated images of the train which they can watch by positioning the graphic novel on their computer's webcam. By moving the book, you can see the engine start up and spit plumes of smoke or make the train go faster or slower, travelling through landscapes and bursting out of the page itself. It remains to be seen if such labour-intensive productions will make a return on the time and expertise invested.

With these advances, or gimmicks, does there come a point when a comic is no longer a comic? What happens when 'motion comics' recycle and convert pre-existing printed comics into limited animation by moving elements of the artwork in layers to suggest depth and movement, perhaps adding some lip-sync simulation? A few motion comics, like *Watchmen*, quirkily retain the balloons and captions alongside the voice-acting, music and sound effects, but most are an entirely audio-visual experience. Does it matter that the reader no longer reads, and the viewer is no longer in constant control of what to take in next? What is clear is that many consumers, especially of America's massive superhero brands, come to these characters first through their much more hyped film, television and game adaptations than through their printed or digital comics, so motion comics may more than satisfy their need for something that resembles a comic. Do you need to read the still, silent graphic novel, when you can watch and hear it?

In this new digital age of comics, the working methods of both writers and artists have also been dramatically changed by computer hardware and software to streamline production. As a result, the profusion of options when working in Illustrator, Photoshop and other programmes can actually make a task more demanding and time-consuming. At their best, a digital colourist-asartist like José Villarrubia has become critical in harnessing the emotive range of different media in their full spectrum, so close to the equivalent analogue media as to be almost indistinguishable. Sampling and collage are delivering astonishing textures and hues, while special computerised effects, such as blurring to emphasise motion or convey extreme close-ups or distance, can make

The Rut
Dave McKean, 2010

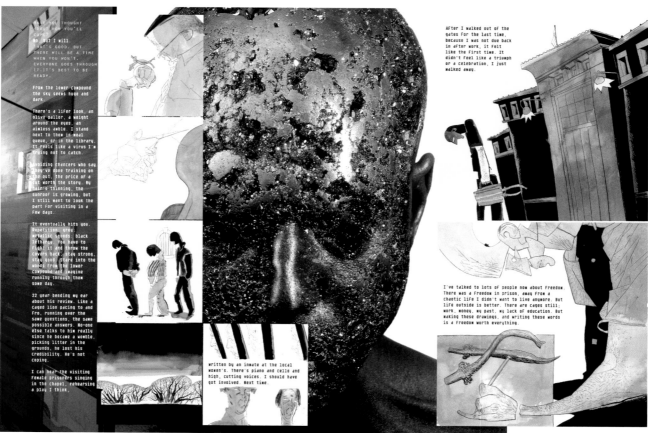

artwork more dramatic. Not everyone, however, appreciates the increased use of computer fonts for lettering. Typesetting in comics always tends to look cold. In the 1960s, Charlton Comics, the most cut-price comic-book publisher in America, simply used a typewriter and credited the lettering to 'A. MacHine'. Hand-lettering in comics, especially solo works, is integral to crafting a seamless whole, pictures and words flowing from the same pen, the same hand. Nevertheless, computerised lettering can be made harmonious, often in a special font based on the artist's handwriting. Sprinkling different forms of the same letter can deceive the eye and prevent texts looking too mechanical.

Parallel and perhaps counter to these digital innovations has been a resurgence of the book as a covetable, tactile object. The quality of design, production values and finish on graphic novels has shot up, largely thanks to a honeymoon period of much lower costs, especially in China. This culminated in 2012 in Chris Ware's *Building Stories*, a large box housing fourteen different printed items, from small single folded strips to a nostalgic, golden-spined hardback, large broadsheets or a sturdy boardgame. Ware wryly commented on the base of his box of tricks, 'With the increasing electronic incorporeality of existence, sometimes it's reassuring – perhaps even necessary – to have something to hold on to.' This sentiment chimes with another

trend towards the application of narrative traditions from the past, some never applied to comics before. To illustrate *Bhimayana: Experiences of Untouchability* (pp.138–9), the biography of Dr Bhimrao Ambedkar, a champion of the rights of the 'untouchable' caste in India and an untouchable himself, the husband-and-wife team of Durgabai and Subhash Vyam were approached to adapt their Pardhan Gond folk art for comics. Refusing to 'force our characters into boxes – it stifles them', the Vyams made their panels sinuous, outlined by *dignas*, decorative borders normally applied to buildings using coloured earth. The Vyams' intense patterning, their faces mainly in profile with large single eyes, and their balloons – bird-like for gentleness, with the mind's eye for thought or a scorpion's sting for venomous dialogue – show how importing such traditions reinvigorates the medium. Another narrative form from India, brightly painted Patua scrolls whose wordless panels are normally accompanied by a live spoken storyteller, has been used in *I See The Promised Land* (2010) by Manu Chitrakar to tell the life story of Martin Luther King Jr, married on the page with the words of African-American performance poet Arthur Flowers. In *Red* (2010), Michael Niucoll Yahgulanaas from the North Pacific Islands of Haida Gwaii has reframed classic Haida imagery and narratives into a manga form, its swirling shapes forming the grid uniting its 108 hand-painted pages. However traditions or technologies transform the evanescent, ever-nascent medium of comics, it will always be the human imagination that is the inexhaustible, infinite canvas.

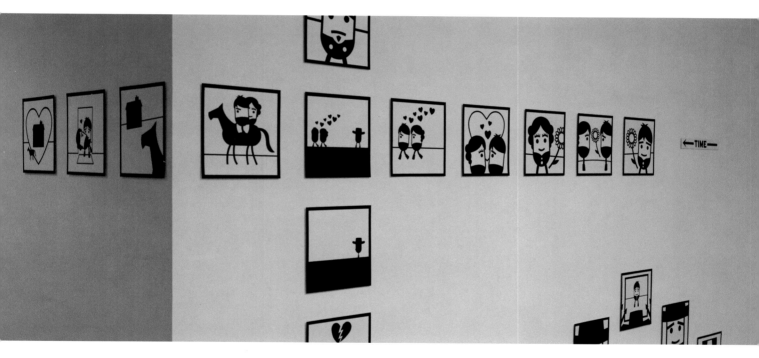

NOTES

1 Encompassing Comics

1 Dylan Horrocks, *Hicksville*, Montreal, Canada, 1998, unpag.
2 Pablo Picasso, *France Soir*, Paris, 14 Oct. 1966.
3 Gregory Steirer, 'The State of Comics Scholarship: Comics Studies and Disciplinarity', *International Journal of Comic Art*, Fall 2011, Drexel Hill, USA, p.276.
4 Salvador Dalí, cited by M. Patinax in 'Les Librairies de bandes dessinées anciennes', *Charlie Mensuel*, no.41 & 42, Paris, 1985.
5 Robert Storr, 'Of Maus and MoMA', *Co-Mix: A Retrospective of Comics, Graphics, and Scraps*, Paris, 2011, p.95.
6 Dylan Horrocks, 'Inventing Comics: Scott McCloud Defines the Form in Understanding Comics', *The Comics Journal*, no.234, Seattle, Washington, June 2001, p.39.

2 Frames of Reference

1 Thierry Smolderen, 'Of Labels, Loops, and Bubbles', *Comic Art*, no.8, Oakland, California, Summer 2006, p.110 & 112. Among other examples pre-dating 'The Yellow Kid' in their use of narrative dialogue balloons in sequential panels, are satirical strips in *The Glasgow Looking Glass* periodical of 1825. See also http://konkykru/earlycomics.html Perhaps the oldest speech balloon , from approximately 650 BC in Pre-Columbian Mesoamerica, was found on the San Andrés cylinder seal and shows a bird 'speaking' a ruler's name joined to its mouth by two lines.
2 Austin Stevens, *Milton Caniff: Conversations*, Jackson, Mississippi, 2002.
3 Renaud Chavanne, *Composition de la bande dessinée*, Paris, 2010.

3 More Than Words Can Say

1 Shaun Tan, interview with Paul Gravett, http://www.paulgravett.com/index.php/articles/article/shaun_tan London, 27 August 2011.

2 Donald Ault, 'Librorum Comicorum Explicatio', *Occident*, no.1 (2nd series), Berkeley, California, 1973, pp.84–8.
3 H.M. Bateman, *Caran d'Ache The Supreme*, London, 1933.
4 Ralph Steadman, 'A Recollection by Ralph Steadman', H.M. Bateman 1887–1970 Centenary Exhibition, exhibition catalogue, London, 1987.
5 *Tatler*, London, 30 November 1923.
6 Dr. Chris Mullen, 'Graphic Novels – The Early Years', exhibition essay, http://www.silentgraphicnovels.com , 2010.
7 Lynd Ward, untitled preface, *Storyteller Without Words: The Wood Engravings of Lynd Ward*, New York, 1974.
8 Art Spiegelman, 'Reading Pictures: A Few Thousand Words on Six Books Without Text', *Lynd Ward: Six Novels in Woodcuts*, New York, 2010.
9 Seth, *Forty Cartoon Books of Interest*, Oakland, California, 2006.
10 Shaun Tan, ibid.

4 Between the Panels

1 Shaun Tan, 'The accidental graphic novelist', *Bookbird: A Journal of International Children's Literature*, no.4, vol.49, Baltimore, Maryland, October 2011, p.8.
2 [George Mikes], *Times Literary Supplement*, London, 29 May 1953.
3 Joe Matt, 'What's the Frequency, Joe?', *Taddle Creek Magazine*, Toronto, Christmas 2002.
4 Donald Ault, ibid.
5 Richard McGuire ,'Here', *Raw*, no.2, vol.2, New York, 1989.

5 Unheard Voices

1 Michael Demson and Heather Brown, *Journal of Graphic Novels and Comics*, no.2, vol.2, Abingdon, Oxon, December 2011, p.155.
2 Art Spiegelman, 'H.K. (R.I.P.)', *New Yorker*, 29 March 1993.

3 Steven Heller, 'The Art of Rebellion', *New York Times*, 6 August 2009.
4 Mohammed Shennawy, interview with Paul Gravett, http://www.paulgravett.com/index.php/articles/article/comics_in_the_middle_east, 22 January 2012.
5 Kate Charlesworth, *New Internationalist*, no.387, Oxford, March 2006.
6 Jogchum Vrielink, 'The Adventures of Tintin in the Land of the Law', http://strasbourgobservers.com/2012/05/02/the-adventures-of-tintin-in-the-land-of-the-law/#_ftn10 , Ghent, Belgium, 2 May 2012,
7 Uncredited, 'Première instance Bruxelles: "Tintin au Congo doit être interdit"', *La Dernière Heure*, http://www.dhnet.be/infos/faits-divers/article/370340/premiere-instance-bruxelles-tintin-au-congo-doit-etre-interdit.html , Brussels, 30 September 2011.
8 Anton Kannemeyer, *du9: l'autre bande dessinée*, http://www.du9.org/en/entretien/anton-kannemeyer-2/ , Paris, September 2012.
9 Marguerite Abouet, 'Drawing on the Universal in Africa: An Interview with Marguerite Abouet', *White River Review*, http://www.wildriverreview.com/interview/drawing-universal-africa/marguerite-abouet/ajayi-angela , Stockton, New Jersey, 2009.

6 First-Persons Singular

1 Lynda Barry, introduction to *The Best American Comics*, Boston, 2008.
2 Waldemar Januszczak, 'A Diet of Bubble and Shriek', *Guardian*, London, 24 July 1984.
3 Justin Green, interview with Shaun Manning, Comic Book Resources website: http://www.comicbookresources.com/?page=article&id=24518 , 22 Jan 2010.
4 Fabrice Neaud, interview with Matthias Wivel, *The Comics Journal* website: http://www.tcj.com/everything-i-do-i-do-at-an-increasing-risk-an-interview-with-fabrice-

CREDITS

neaud/, 11 April 2011.

5 Lynda Barry, 'A Conversation with Lynda Barry' by Elissa Shappell, *Tin House*, no.29, Portland, Oregon, Fall 2006.

6 Patrice Killoffer, *Collection* no.2, En Marge, Montreuil, France, April 2011.

7 The Human Touch

1 Thierry Groensteen, *The System of Comics*, p.17–18, Jackson, Mississippi, 2009.

2 Woodrow Phoenix, interview with Dan Berry, The Comics Bureau: http:// thecomicsbureau.co.uk/2010/12/woodrow-phoenix-interview/ , 9 December 2010.

3 Seth, 'Poetry, Design and Comics: An Interview with Seth' by Marc Ngui, *Carousel* vol.19, Toronto, Spring-Summer 2006.

4 Jules Feiffer, *Backing into Forward*, p.62, New York, 2010.

8 Infinite Canvases

1 Eric Monster Millikin, interviewed by Robert J. Beck: http://www.lotsofinterviews.com/#/wcseric-monster-milikin/4537549372 , 13 December 2009.

2 Josh Neufeld, *SMITH Magazine* Blog: http://www.smithmag.net/afterthedeluge/2009/08/24/bells/, 24 August 2009.

3 Dave McKean, Commentary on Club Salsa, [accessed 12 February 2013] : http://www.netcontrol.net/archives-98/226028/index.shtml , 29 January 1996.

4 Scott McCloud, *Reinventing Comics*, New York, 2000.

5 Matt Madden, 'Oubapo: Comics and Constraints from France', Words Without Borders: http://wordswithoutborders.org/article/oubapo-article1#ixzz2KjLASEJL , February 2013.

6 Antony Johnston, 'After Days of Passion: Tragedy/Gothic Mystery': http://www.antonyjohnston.com/titles/passion/, 2001.

Images are copyright the creator/s unless stated otherwise

p.7 © Private Collection

p.11 Published by Jonathan Cape. Reprinted by permission of The Random House Group Limited

p.14–15 © Martin Vaughn-James, courtesy Coach House Books (1975, 2013) and Les Impressions Nouvelles (2006)

p.17 © 1955 William-M Gaines, Agent, Inc., reprinted with permission. All rights reserved

p.19 Kirby Museum's Digital Archive, with thanks to Mike Burkey (original art) and Greg Theakston (photocopy), © 2013 Marvel

p.20 © Jorge Fidel Alvarez / 9 eme Art+

p.21 Courtesy Heritage Auctions / HA.com

p.23 © Deutsche Comicforschung, from *Seicherls Weltreise*, from a special issue of *Das Kleine Blatt* 1934 or 1935

p.24 Courtesy Library of Congress Prints and Photographs Division, Washington DC. Photoprint copyrighted by Elizabeth Alice Austen

p.25 Courtesy San Francisco Academy of Comic Art Collection, The Ohio State University Billy Ireland Cartoon Library & Museum

p.27 Courtesy Heritage Auctions/HA.com. Terry & The Pirates characters, names and related indicia are trademarks of and © TMS News and Features LLC

p.30 Courtesy Anne Opotowsky, Aya Morton, Gestalt Publishing

p.31 Kaori Moru & EnterBrain Inc. Tokyo – via the Tuttle-Mori Agency Inc. © 2009, Kaoru Mori

pp.32–3 Seth & Sarah McMahon Fold-Out from *George Sprott* (2009) by Seth published by Drawn & Quarterly

p.35 © Punch Limited

p.37 © DACS 2013 / Artists Rights Society, New York / VG Bild-Kunst, Bonn

p.39 From *Vertigo* by Lynd Ward, by permission of Robin Ward Savage and Nanda Weedon Ward

p.41 Courtesy Lothian Books / Hachette

p.46 © Marion Fayolle & Editions Michel Legarde & Nobrow

p.49 © Jon McNaught & Nobrow

p.50 © Guy Delcourt Productions, 2011

p.60 Courtesy Archivio Crepax, Galleria Nuages, Milan, and Galerie Champaka, Brussels

p.61 © De Luca / Traverso

p.63 © 2013 Marvel

p.67 Courtesy Guy Delcourt Productions, 2004

p.71 © Robert Crumb, 1989. Used with permission of Robert Crumb, c/o Agence Litteraire Lora Fountain & Associates

p.76 © Estate of Garrett Whyte

p.77 © Estate of Jackie Ormes, courtesy Nancy Goldstein © Nancy Goldstein

p.81 © 2010 by Aristophane. Reprinted by permission of First Second Books, an imprint of Roaring Brook Press, a division of Holtzbrinck Publishing Holdings Limited Partnership. All rights reserved

p.83 © 2006 Gene Yang. Reprinted by permission of First Second Books, an imprint of Roaring Brook Press, a division of Holtzbrinck Publishing Holdings Limited Partnership. All rights reserved

P.88 © Estate of Charlotte Salomon / Charlotte Salomon Foundation / Anton Kras. Courtesy the Jewish Historical Museum Collection, Amsterdam

p.90 © Estate of Keiji Nakazawa / Leonard Rifas, courtesy Last Gasp Publishing, San Francisco

p.91 © Justin Green, courtesy Last Gasp Publishing, San Francisco

p.93 © 2000 Fabrice Neaud and Ego Comme X

p.99 © 2009 Emmanuel Guibert. Reprinted by permission of First Second Books, an imprint of Roaring Brook Press, a division of Holtzbrinck Publishing Holdings Limited Partnership. All rights reserved

p.101 *Judith Forest* (William Henne, Xavier Löwenthal and Thomas Boivin)

p.103 © Carol Tyler, courtesy Fantagraphics

p.109 © Shigeru Mizuki / Mizuki Production, courtesy Drawn & Quarterly

p.111 © Woodrow Phoenix and Myriad Editions, published by Myriad Editions 2008

p.117 © Alex Barbier – FRMK 2011

p.118 © Moebius Productions

p.127 'Chère Patagonie' by Jorge Gonzalez © Dupuis 2011

INDEX

INDEX